Soccer Mastery

The little things that make a big difference:

Habits, Secrets and Strategies that will escalate your game to the next level

Chest Dugger

Contents

ABOUT THE AUTHOR 6

DISCLAIMER 8

Introduction 9

When a Butterfly Flaps its Wings in Mongolia......................... 13

The Game Today – How Little Things Have Changed the Soccer Story 17

VAR – Talking Points or Getting Accurate Results? 22

Shock Horror – Players Discover that Eight Pints of Beer and a Bag of Fries is NOT the Perfect Post Match Meal 26

Playing at Capacity – Player Analytics................................. 28

Never Stifle a Sniff – Be Ready for Offensive Opportunities ... 30

Assessing Our Opponents To Maximize Scoring Opportunities.... 30

The Advantages of Being a Two Footed Striker 34

Making the Step Over, Drop of the Shoulder and Other Dribbling Tricks a Natural Part of Our Game.................................... 40

Making the Most of the Midfield.................................... 48

Making the Ball Our Friend 49

Tactical Awareness – Keeping Shape and Making Runs 57

Becoming a Dream of a Defensive Player 59

No Longer a Player Apart – The Goalkeeper 59

Mr Reliability, Mrs Trustworthy, Master Mindful 64

The Organiser 66

Making the Striker Pay the Penalty 70

Playing For Time – Know the Rules 74

The Stopper Dies, The Playmaker is Born 76

The Technical Areas on Which a Center Back Needs to Work 77

It's All in the Mind 81

Let's Get Physical 83

Finding Our Life Partner 86

Tactical Awareness in Defense 88

The Attacking Defender 89

Dealing With A Wizard of the Wing 93

Physical Fitness..95

It's All In The Mind 106

The Different Aspects to Mental Toughness.................................109

Some Simple Ways to Develop Mental Strength 114

Learning From the Best 120

Choosing Our Role Model 120

Strikers 121

Midfielders 123

Defense 125

Conclusion 129

ABOUT THE AUTHOR

Chest Dugger is a pen name for our soccer coaching team, Abiprod. Abiprod is a team of passionate professional coaches and fans, based in UK and Australia.

We have been fans of the beautiful game for decades, coaching junior and senior teams. Like every soccer fan around the globe, we watch and play the beautiful game as much as we can. Whether we're fans of Manchester United, Real Madrid, Arsenal or LA Galaxy; we share a common love for the beautiful game.

Through our experiences, we've noticed that there's very little information for the common soccer fan who wants to escalate his game to the next level. Or get their kids started on the way. This is especially the case for those who live outside Europe and South America. Expensive soccer coaching and methodology is pretty rare in even rich countries like USA and Australia.

Being passionate about the game, we want to get the message across to as many people as possible. Through our soccer coaching blog, books and products; we aim to bring the best of soccer coaching to the world. Though we are starting off in USA and Australia, anyone who's passionate about the beautiful game can use our tactics and strategies.

You can find a link to our other books <u>here</u>.

DISCLAIMER

Introduction

Think of Britain for a moment. Good old Blighty across the waves. What comes to mind? Rain? Red buses? Overcooked food? Amazing theatre and brilliant sport?

The last of these is, in many ways, down to another British obsession – the cup of tea. Brits have always enjoyed a cuppa; right back in the seventeenth century even. There's no better way for a chinwag (and there's an evocative term for a small gathering and a sharing of views) than to have it around a cup of tea.

The thing is, though, that for tea to be the flavorsome brew the Brits know and love, it has to be made from boiled water. Now, by happy chance, boiling water has a second effect beyond making a lovely drink. It kills bacteria.

It was from eliminating such infection in their water supplies that Britons were able to become healthier. And a healthy population encourages the development of an economy.

So Britain became a prosperous nation, and that gave it the framework to enter the industrial revolution. It was, as we shall see later, as a direct result of that economic change that the game of soccer emerged. It grew from an informal and lawless jumble of violent conflicts into a properly regulated sport. Previously, its existence was largely limited to a way of tempering the testosterone trickling out of teenagers in the country's poshest schools, It was thanks to the industrial revolution that clubs, and then leagues, became formalized.

Thus, when we are watching the final of the World Cup, or visiting a pulsating stadium with our kids, or having a kick around in park we can thank **the humble cup of tea** for what we are enjoying. Now, there's a good reason to put the kettle on.

Fortunately (or not, depending on your point of view) this is neither a book about the Industrial Revolution nor even the relatively mundane but many faceted drink that is tea. Instead, it is a book that will look at the everyday actions we can take that will lead us to become even better soccer players.

It gives an insight into the many hacks which turn us into stronger players, or more accomplished coaches. Some of these tips have their origins in happy accidents. They are the unintended outcomes which lead, inadvertently, to improvements in our lives. Or, more importantly (we would argue, with our tongue firmly in our cheeks) in our knowledge of and ability to play soccer.

We will look at the secrets, habits and strategies that will enhance our abilities on the pitch – whether playing or coaching. We will consider the factors which aid our understanding of the game, and therefore our enjoyment of it. We will consider the three major departments of the game; offense, midfield and defense. We will look at tactical elements of the game. Skills such as first touch, dribbling and shooting will be discussed.

This book will offer tips and tactics for young players, and also for those who might not retain the athleticism that they used to. We will look at the physical and mental training we can fit into our lives to make us better athletes, and thus better soccer players.

But let's begin with a bit of context. As the great Liverpool manager, Bill Shankly, once said in a somewhat paraphrased fashion: 'Football is much more than a matter of life and death.' So we will take a brief look at the importance of the random outcomes of life, how the unexpected follows from an unrelated action. We will use this principle as a guide to taking advantage of everyday events in our quest to become soccer masters.

Our book will provide tips, strategies, hacks and habits we can use to improve our soccer technique and play. We will also offer thirty top tips which support and develop the numerous hints and drills we outline in the main part of the book. We will even highlight a number of the young players lighting up every position of the English Premier League, the most widely available top level soccer we can find on US TV.

When a Butterfly Flaps its Wings in Mongolia...

...it causes a tornado in Wyoming.

Well, it doesn't. But decisions, big and small, can have consequences well beyond those that are expected.

Did Admiral Yamamoto have the slightest inkling that his idea to launch an attack on Pearl Harbor would lead to the world's existence standing on a knife edge? That it would preface the Cold War, McCarthyism and the growth of communism across Eastern Europe? That it would result in the total destruction of two Japanese cities, Nagasaki and, before this, Hiroshima?

Or when Patrick McDonald set up a food stand in Los Angeles it would result in golden arches shaped like M's bestriding just about every down town, shopping mall and retail park across the developed world?

Not every unintentional outcome is disastrous – not that we are suggesting that is the case with McDonald's. After all, most of the readers of this book will be sports players, or at least people with an interest in soccer. What can be better than preparing for a game with a Big Mac, or celebrating a victory with a super-sized chocolate milk shake? (As we will see, it was not that long ago that such a post-match meal was common place)

Let's look at another instance. When Paul Simon was cast as the White Rabbit in his school's production of Alice in Wonderland there was no real suggestion that he might find a like minded musical type in the same production. It just happened to be the case that a certain Arthur Garfunkel was playing the part of the Cheshire cat.

Even then, these two might not have achieved the mega status they did had not a music producer experimented with adding a background track to a fine, but little played track called 'The Sound of Silence'. Of course, since those days, Paul Simon went on to record not just one but two seminal record albums of the entire globe – Bridge Over Troubled Water and Graceland. The latter of these played an enormous part in bringing the culture of black South Africa to a worldwide audience.

As such, it played it's part in ensuring the atrocity of apartheid was placed under the scrutiny of nations who previously might shake their heads, make a tutting noise and get on with cleaning the car. Instead, Graceland inspired debate, not all of it positive (there was misplaced talk of exploitation of black musicians, something totally unjustified) and ultimately played its part in helping South Africa become a major world force.

But what if his teacher back in elementary school had chosen some other play; or CS Lewis had not have been strangely obsessed by Alice Liddell and stuck to mathematics rather than writing Alice in Wonderland? Everything has its consequences, and frequently they are not planned.

There is a word for these happy accidents. Serendipity. When James Naismith was annoyed to find the peach basket empty at the hostel in which he was staying in 1891 he could have just gone hungry. Instead, he decided to appease his annoyance by throwing footballs into it, and basketball was born.

But these are all unplanned outcomes. What we will look at in this book are the sort of consequences we might expect if we follow a certain path of actions. It is not too great an intellectual leap to reach conclusions such as that an investment in education will improve chances for young people; or even a gradual disillusionment with traditional politics plants the seeds for the election of a President such as Donald Trump.

Still, here, we are looking at much more important matters than politics or education. We are looking at ways to make ourselves, our teams, our kids into better soccer players. The sort of small, everyday changes we can make, or adapt to our own circumstances, which will help us to become masters of the game. At least, masters in relation to our own levels of ability.

And we will start by taking a look back at the evolution of soccer to the stage at which it became recognizable as the sport we play, whether professionally, for a weekend team, a youth side or even just a kick about in the park. Because, as we will see, it is only due to a number of unplanned actions that the game even exists today. Now those actions were serendipitous indeed.

The Game Today – How Little Things Have Changed the Soccer Story

Picture the scene. The late Autumn sun shines. There is a chill in the air, but that is alleviated when sunshine strikes us directly. Nearby, the River Thames glitters, wide and slow moving. Look up, and in the distance the Norman edifice that is Windsor Castle stands tall and impregnable. It is astonishing that so unutterably English a scene should be overlooked by a stronghold built in an age when a Frenchman ruled the country. Back in the time of the building of Windsor Castle Britain was ruled by the French - today the French rule the world, in the soccer sense at least. William the Conqueror surpassed by Kylian M'Bappe.

Bear with us here, we are getting to the point we want to make. It might take a paragraph or two yet. Back to Windsor, the poshest town in the poshest county of England, Berkshire. Behind us, tall windows light stately buildings. Small boys pass, dressed in long tailcoats, waistcoats and grey bags. An occasional adult, attired in a smart white bow tie, with black jacket and striped trousers, passes. The boys defer to these larger versions of themselves.

Those with good hearing and a nosy nature might hear unbroken voices pipe 'He's a fine beak,' or other such compliment.

Have we travelled in time, back to some Victorian era of tailcoats and top hats? A large Boeing 747, undercarriage down on its descent into Heathrow airport, puts paid to that theory. Nearby we spy a gap in the wall; a portered kiosk prevents unwelcome visitors from entering the privileged internal workings of this place. At least, until the summer falls and the tail coated youngsters have fled for the private yachts and luxurious villas of their parents. But if we were allowed, we could head into the cloistered square through the guarded metal gate, and make our way to a long wall.

Once there we would hear voices, more manly in pitch than before, but still youthful sounding. Soon we would find a narrow strip of turf on which larger boys are fighting over a spherical object. One is on all fours, the ball between his legs; others appear engaged in the sort of free for all more often found in a tough city center when the night club closes and inebriated young men and women alternately vomit and fight in the streets. The uniform of those young Brits is short skirts and white T shirts, low slung blouses and blue jeans. The youngsters we see now may come from homes of greater opportunity than their partying peers, but the boys here still have their own form of uniform; tight white trousers tucked into long socks and baggy striped shirts.

In fact, despite suggestions to the contrary, we are not caught in some historical time lapse; we are firmly in 2019 but we are watching an event with a strong tie to history. One that is unchanged for more than two centuries. We are at Eton College, the school for toffs and sons of earls and aristocrats. They are playing the Wall Game and we are looking at one of the earliest forms of the world's most popular game; we are watching the genesis of soccer.

In fact, some historians date the game back to ancient Chinese dynasties from more than 2000 years ago. The game re-emerged from time to time, mostly in Britain, and was frequently banned for the 'sinful' feelings it encouraged. (Nothing changes, as fans watching any local derby will attest). Then, as the traditional English public schools gained popularity, something was needed to keep the infatigable energy of several hundred adolescents in check.

Various options were considered and dismissed. Hunting would eliminate wildlife for miles around, leaving nothing to occupy fathers in need of their own sport. Declaring war on France was always a good option, but like the best things in life, was most appreciated in moderation. Beating up the local townsfolk, smashing their windows and stealing their wares was undoubtedly fun (and the victims were poor, so did not really matter) but somehow that was not quite cricket, a worst sin than murder (although it was a largely acceptable past time at Harrow College!)

So ball games developed. Mostly, in the early days, they involved kicking (occasionally the ball), wrestling and other homo erotic past times which have their origin in the alma maters of the privileged youth of Britain. Then, young master Webb Ellis was about to be dispossessed (or more likely, back then, decapitated) at Rugby School during a game of footie (sometimes known as 'kill the small boy'). Faced with a choice between being kicked to death by his opponents or beaten on the bare backside by his peers (for costing them the game, and the honor of the house) he picked up the football and ran with it. Laws being not quite developed then, nobody was sure what to do.

Should Webb Ellis be roasted in front of the Prefects' fire for his sins? Sent down for cheating? Given iconic status for inventing a new game? Well, the last came to fruition, no doubt to the relief of the young rascal. Rugby was born, and that one small act – **picking up the ball rather than kicking it** – ultimately led directly to the sport of soccer we know today.

Because it became apparent that laws were needed. No longer would the pitch be the size of whatever field came to hand; the number of players on each team would be capped by a set number rather than the number of boys not being fed cod liver oil by Matron in the Sick Bay. The game, in the loosest possible way, began to take shape.

Soon, and not too far away, Mr. Darby was deciding that a nice bridge made of iron would look scenic over the River Severn. Others were seeing the opportunities created by pumping the atmosphere full of carbon dioxide and mighty furnaces were built. Britain was going through the industrial revolution, factories were going up and people we moving from rat filled country cottages to tiny terraced housing cramped together under the fug of chimney smoke. From plague to purgatory, it might be said.

Once more, soccer came to the rescue. It wasn't testosterone this time that needed to be burned away, but the frustrations of living packed together like fun seekers queuing for a ride on a Disney World rollercoaster in high summer. So the factory owners took their lead from the public schools to which their children aspired, built stadia and founded soccer teams. It started in Sheffield, a harsh city in the industrial north, and soon spread.

A sad little by note – Notts County were one of the first clubs to be formed. They came about in 1862, one of the new sources of recreation, a by product of the industrial revolution. Their few forbears soon disappeared but Notts County survived – never thrived, but lived on, a source of pride to their small number of East Midlands supporters. They won the FA Cup in 1894, and were runners up in the Anglo Italian Cup (that bastion of soccer excellence, sadly no more) in 1994. In between, the odd lower league title filtered their way. Notts County are now the oldest professional league side in the world. By the time you read this, that probably won't be true as it seems highly likely that they will fall out of the bottom tier of English League Soccer, Division Two, and enter the world of non-league stalwarts. A shame.

So there, in two halves of 800 words or so, we have a potted history of the origins of soccer. But of course, the world's greatest game is developing all of the time. That is how it retains its supremacy. Each change in the law of the game, each tactical innovation, each small step of progress in the way players look after themselves, each development moves soccer forwards. Or, cynics might argue, backwards. But however we regard them, these developments change the way we play.

Let us take three innovations as an example. The introduction of VAR; the changing role nutrition plays in a soccer player's make up and the growing use of player analytics.

VAR – Taking Out the Talking Points or Getting Accurate Results?

About three days before writing this page, there was an important match in the English Premier League. Cardiff City were hosting Chelsea. With just a few games to go before the end of the season, both teams had plenty to play for: Cardiff were in the relegation zone, but a victory would move them to within two points of the safety zone with a game in hand. Chelsea, having enjoyed years of success, are beginning to struggle now that Roman Abramovich's cash is less free flowing. They were desperate for a victory to keep them in touch for a top four finish. That would provide their best chance to secure Champions' League soccer next season, with all its associated millions of television cash and gate receipts.

The best players in the world want to play Champions' League football, and each season away from the competition would see Chelsea falling behind the elite teams in the English Premier League as the biggest players on the planet choose the likes of Juventus, Bayern Munich, Dortmund, Liverpool and Athletico Madrid over the west London blues. (Causing, we might conclude, west London blues).

But at the time of the match, neither Chelsea nor Cardiff was in great form. There was no surprise, then, that it was a dour game between two sides struggling for confidence. But slowly, surprisingly perhaps, Cardiff began to get on top. They scored, and with only a few minutes left it really seemed like they would hold on. Then Chelsea got a corner. Picture the scene; Cardiff have lined up zonally, with their defense spread along the six yard line. They have not left players on the posts. Chelsea have two players around the Cardiff keeper.

As the corner is taken, these two players are maybe four or five yards 'offside' – although, because it is a corner, they are not.

The delivery is an out swinger, and a Chelsea player heads the ball goalward from the edge of the six yard box. There is no doubt about this. Meanwhile, Cesar Azpilicueta, the Chelsea full back who was one of the players surrounding the Cardiff keeper, has moved back towards the six yard box. At the point of the ball being flicked on, he is two, perhaps three, yards offside.

Unmarked, he nods the ball into the net. The Cardiff players look towards the referee and his assistant. The goal is so ludicrously offside that their keeper is already looking to take the free kick. With astonishment, then disbelief, then absolute fury they see both the referee and his linesman (sorry, assistant referee – there's a silly name if ever there was one) heading back to the half way line. A goal is given.

It is a goal that will probably send Cardiff out of the premier league, costing the club maybe two hundred million dollars in lost revenue, lost TV money and smaller crowds. It will almost certainly result in the manager being replaced at the end of the season. It could push Chelsea to a top four finish, and cost the club who should rightfully have finished above them perhaps $50 million in lost Champions' League funding.

All because a referee and his assistant make the most appalling of mistakes. After the game, the TV analysts and pundits tried to explain the error. They could not do so. Their best offer was that the assistant allowed himself to become unsighted as the corner taker stepped in front of him. But this was an unsatisfactory excuse. The goal scorer could never have been onside given his starting position.

VAR (video assistant referee) would remove this kind of error. Already widely in use across the major leagues of Europe and a feature of the recent Russian World Cup, it reduces refereeing errors. It is not perfect; one issue is deciding when it should be used. To review every decision would be to slow the game down to such an extent that it loses its appeal as a spectator sport. Therefore, somebody has to decide when to inform the referee that he or she has made an error.

Sometimes VAR gets it wrong as well. Just like Hawk-eye in tennis, it is a fallible system – just less fallible than the human eye. So how does VAR change the professional game?

Perhaps the biggest way is in cleaning up low level foul play in the penalty area. Now, a defender who grabs an arm to prevent an opponent from jumping – a striker who falls, untouched, to ground will be exposed. It means that corners, free kicks and so forth will became more a contest of skill than a game of chance around who can hoodwink the referee. Surely, that can only be a good (if not perfect) improvement?

Finally, there are some who complain that VAR will, and has, taken the joy of talking about contentious issues out of the game. But this argument holds little water. Ask the Nigerian team, or its supporters, after it failed to get a penalty at the World Cup when the Argentinian Marcus Rojo handled the ball. Or the fans of Croatia when, in the final no less, what appeared to be a dive from Antoine Griezmann was not reviewed because it did not meet the criteria for VAR to look at it. France scored from the resultant free kick.

Top Tip To Take-Away 1 – For the overwhelming majority of us who play the game at an amateur level, VAR will never become a part of our playing lives. If professional referees and their linesmen get it wrong, then amateur ones certainly will. Playing an offside trap is legitimate, but a very risky tactic at the amateur levels of the game.

Shock Horror – Players Discover that Eight Pints of Beer and a Bag of Fries is NOT the Perfect Post Match Meal

True soccer aficionados will know of the great manager Brian Clough. Clough was a tricky customer – outspoken and opinionated. But as a coach he was capable of taking mediocre players to astonishing heights. After a successful playing career was cut short by an injury – he may well have been a part of the 1966 World Cup winning team had he recovered – he went into management.

In the mid-sixties, he took his first job as coach at the highly unfashionable lower league team Hartlepool United. Here, he took the term 'coach' literally, taking a driving test which allowed him to steer the team literally as well as metaphorically. He oversaw the purchase of an old bus and became the club's coach driver, since Hartlepool United were far too small a team to hire such transport on a regular basis. For all his mastery of tactics, team building and man management, the new coach knew nothing about nutrition. Clough would stop off on the way home from away matches and buy the team fish and chips. A perfect way to replace carbohydrate and re-energize muscles. Or, perhaps, not.

At the other end of the spectrum of soccer playing talent, there was a heavy drinking culture within the British game in the latter half of the twentieth century. That was as true in the top divisions of English and Scottish soccer as it was down in the lower reaches of the game. While soccer players in Europe already understood the science of nutrition as a way of supporting performance, and the North American Soccer League was, to be fair, still a relatively unprofessional set up, players in the UK liked a pint. Or ten.

Even a great such as Tony Adams – England and Arsenal captain, double winner and defensive stalwart par excellence – had no idea how to look after himself. In his autobiography, Addicted, Adams explains how he would train wearing a plastic bin liner to sweat the alcohol out of his system.

He would go on long binge drinking sessions, leading to the ignominy of wetting himself. On one occasion, he was even drunk while playing in a league match; he describes the embarrassment of trying to run down the wing and just falling over.

Adams, fortunately, faced up to his alcoholism and continues to overcome it (alcoholics are keen to point out that they are never cured). Not least in encouraging him to this state was the French manager Arsene Wenger, who joined Arsenal as coach in the mid-1990s, and introduced a regime which paid close attention to diet.

If VAR is never likely to have an impact on the level at which most of us play (it seems unlikely there will be cameras and monitors set up on the local park pitches) then diet certainly can. Good diet enables us to train harder, to stay fitter, to recover more quickly and to play at a higher pace in matches. It is a subject to which we will return later.

Top Tip To Take-Away 2 – As amateur players, it is not practical to base our lives around the nutritional needs of professional soccer players, but we can still eat carefully and drink in moderation. That will help our all round health as well as our performance on the turf of kings. It will significantly increase our quality of life outside of soccer.

Playing at Capacity – Player Analytics

Just as with diet, analytics are something that can be used – to a relative degree - at any level of the game to improve performance. Fundamentally analytics in the sense we are applying here measure player capacity, and help tune soccer players to reach that capacity. At higher levels, they also allow coaches to make informed judgements about substitutions.

For example, a player who can sustain twelve kilometers of running (the average, at professional level, is a little under 11 km) will begin to fade once that point is reached. A coach will know that, however well that player is performing, his standard will fall as tiredness creeps in. That deterioration will include mental standards as well as physical ones.

So, for example, a midfielder who has already been shown a yellow card and who has exceeded their normal running capacity is more likely to misjudge a tackle and earn the second yellow that translates into a red. A coach might therefore choose to remove the player for this reason. The crowd, having seen their hero perform excellently, might be bemused by the decision. The coach, though, will have the analytics on hand, and will have made his judgement call based on evidence.

The result of analytics is that substitutions influence games more often, and players avoid injuries more often as these most often occur when a player is physically and mentally tired.

Top Tip To Take-Away 3 – There are plenty of books around that examine the role of analytics in the modern game. Some, like one by your author Chest Dugger, focus on the ways analytics can support the amateur player as well as top professionals. Such a book is worth a read, for coaches as well as players. You can find that book here.

So far, we have looked at changes – in soccer and beyond – that are broad in their nature. Now we will move on to the even more small, and more precise, changes that can influence us as players at our own level. We will use examples from the professional game to illustrate our points where possible. However, these chapters will offer practical ideas to make us better players.

Never Stifle a Sniff – How To Be Ready for Offensive Opportunities

Being a top striker is all about instinct. It is about being in the right place at the right time, and having the speed of thought and movement to take advantage of that judgement (or good fortune…although, there is plenty of truth in the saying that the best players make their own luck). Good offensive players find themselves in the correct spot far too often for it to be down to chance. They score too often for their finishing to be down to luck.

While we might never get to play on the world stage, or coach stars of the future, we can still improve our offensive abilities through things we do in our everyday lives.

Assessing Our Opponents To Maximize Scoring Opportunities

A pre-requisite for being a good striker is self confidence. We need to feel that we are going to take chances, put away that snap opportunity. We also need well-honed skills, strong technique and good communication.

But there is another factor which can be overlooked, even by the best coaches and the most able finishers. That is to **neutralize the strength of the opposition.** It is here that we will offer our next worthwhile hack to make us better soccer players.

A good question to start with is to ask why a particular player is in the team? In other words, what are their strengths? Sergio Ramos, the Real Madrid center back is there because he is a dominant leader and a no-nonsense tackler. He has no obvious weaknesses (as we might expect from a seasoned international who plays for one of the world's leading clubs), but those are his strengths.

Other defenders might be blessed with stunning pace or with great positional sense (Bobby Moore, perhaps the finest center back of all time, seemed to have the remarkable ability to always be in the right place. It meant that he was already three quarters of the way to dispossessing his opponent or blocking a shot before he had to put his body on the line.)

Taking a defender such as Virgil Van Dijk, the Dutch center half who many would describe as the world's best at the moment, we have a problem. Because he possesses all of those attributes. And is also good in the air. Certainly, at the level we play we are not going to come across a Ramos or Moore or Van Dijk; though we will come up against players who are equally dominant within their standard of the game.

So, in deciding 'why' a player is in a team, we make our assessment as quickly as we can. It helps if we have already played against the club, and are familiar with their back four (or three, or five), but usually within five to ten minutes we can gather a picture of our opponent. Does he or she favor one foot over the other? Do they like to push forward and leave gaps behind them?

We then consider our own strengths, and seek to match these against the opposing defender who will find it most difficult to deal with those attributes we possess. This is easiest to do as coach, because in that role we have the authority to set up our team. We can put our pacy winger against the slower full back, or send our number ten into the area frequently abandoned by a marauding center half.

As player, it is more difficult. Here, we have to consider not only our own performance but also our role in the team. However, we will still contribute more to our overall team effectiveness if we have the biggest opportunity to make an impact.

We can see this tactical move played excellently if we look on line for highlights of Arsenal v Manchester Utd in the 2019 English FA cup. It was a tactical masterclass from the young Manchester United manager, Ole Gunnar Solskjaer.

Spotting that Arsenal's main threat came from their full backs getting forward, he left two fast strikers – the English youngster Marcus Rashford and Belgian powerhouse Romalu Lukaku forward and wide.

Solskjaer, who had scored the winning goal when United won the Champions League in 1999, then packed his defense and waited for an Arsenal attack to break down. His team simply then broke quickly, distributing the ball wide to one of their strikers who always seemed to be in space. With a speedy supporting midfielder in tow, the wide striker broke forward, drew a slower center half out of position and played the ball into the central area.

In terms of the game, Arsenal dominated possession and pressure. But in terms of the result, Manchester United won comfortably.

Even at the level at which we play, we can develop that flexibility of mind to both spot the strengths and weaknesses of an opponent and exploit them to maximum effect. Post practice analysis, half time team talks, drills in training sessions and even simply getting used to analyzing people in our everyday lives makes this sort of tactical awareness second nature.

And what can be more fun than thinking up the weaknesses of our work opponents...sorry, I mean colleagues, and thinking up ways to exploit them? We all like to do it, don't we?

Top Tip To Take-Away 4 – A rapid analysis of our opponents' strengths and weaknesses can help us to make our own performances more effective.

Top Tip To Take-Away 5 – Coaches have the over-view of the team performance, players should fit into the team strategy. Players can (and should) seek to use their own initiative during a game, but not to the detriment of the overall team play.

The Advantages of Being a Two Footed Striker

We mentioned Virgil Van Dijk above, and will now return to him. Don't worry, this book won't turn into a tribute to the biggest Dutch master since Vincent Van Gogh realized he could draw a sunflower, however much his play at the moment deserves it.

Lots of readers will get their main access to top level soccer from watching the English Premier League. It makes sense therefore, when we illustrate our suggestions with real life examples, we reference this league where possible. (Which is not to say that other leagues do not produce as high quality soccer or players, it is just that they can be harder to access on American TV.)

So back to VVD (as he is widely referred to on Twitter). The example we will use is a crucial match towards the end of the 2018-19 season. Liverpool need to win to resume their place at the top of the table – defeat means they remain a point behind Manchester city and will have played a game more. Their opponents, Tottenham Hotspurs, are battling to stay in the top four and secure champions league entry.

The scores are level and Liverpool are pressing hard when they lose possession. With a quick interchange of passes Tottenham break into the Reds' half, and find themselves in a classic two v one situation. The pacy Frenchman Sissoko is on the ball, and the equally quick Korean Heung Min Son is in support. Son is having a terrific season, and if he finds himself in a one on one situation with the Liverpool keeper all bets on whether he converts the chance will be off.

As last defender, the aforementioned Van Dijk has a problem. Move into to tackle Sissoko, and the ball will be passed to the speeding Son, who will be in that much wanted one v one situation with the keeper. Hold off and prevent the pass and Sissoko will have a shooting opportunity.

The defending which ensues is magical. Van Dijk positions himself to prevent the pass, but is also close enough to keep the ball on Sissoko's weaker foot. The striker shoots from the edge of the box, but his effort lacks confidence and ends up high and wide in the stand behind the goal.

Brilliant. Liverpool go on to win the game and head back to the top of the league.

But, quite reasonably, we might think that as impressive as VVD might be, this is a chapter on offensive moves. Which is true. Our point is that had Sissoko been able to shoot with his left foot as accurately as he normally does with his right, then the net might have been absorbing the ball, rather than some poor fan behind the goal catching one in the face.

It is rare for a player to be genuinely two footed. One leg does normally dominate. However, it is possible – with practice and determination – to get that weaker limb working well enough for it not to be a handicap.

Coaches and parents of young kids have a big responsibility here. Junior players find it hard to see the importance of long term improvement. It is all about the 'now' in their psyche. Therefore, they will use their dominant foot whenever possible, because that gives them greater short term success.

In doing so, they are committing a number of soccer sins. They are widening the gap between the strengths of their dominant and weaker foot. That, in turn, will encourage even less use of the weaker side.

They are also losing their natural – if less developed – balance on their weaker side, because they are not using it. Finally, psychologically they are reinforcing their sense of the relative strength and weakness of their two feet. That will further discourage use of the weaker limb.

But coaches and parents can help to address this with lots of drills where the weaker foot has to be used. These can be lots of fun, because players struggle with these drills, so amusing things happen. Soon, though, if they have worked hard, they will be able to use both feet instinctively. Probably, one foot will always be dominant, but at least the player will be confident on both sides.

Which Sissoko clearly was not. And he's a top standard professional.

But for most of us, it is too late to develop our weaker foot naturally, as children do. We have reached the age where it always feels a little awkward to use our weaker peg for anything more than standing on, or at a squeeze making an unpressured ten yard pass.

Equally, though, we can still learn to improve the weaker foot. Practice is as important for us as it is for young players, but as we get older, we are also more able to examine technique, learn it and then apply it in match situations.

The technique for shooting remains broadly the same whichever foot is used. It is just that it comes more naturally with the stronger foot. However, this rule of thumb is itself a little misleading. Because the non-kicking foot is as important as the one which strikes the ball when shooting. If the position of this foot is incorrect, then balance will be wrong and control is lost.

When we are struggling to make our body feel more natural as we try to shoot with our weaker foot, we can tell ourselves that it is only the roles that have swapped, not the importance attached to them.

Our non-kicking foot is planted firmly to the side of the ball. We strike smoothly through the ball, hitting it with the laces (for power) or side foot for accuracy. Our head goes forward over the ball, keeping it low. Nearly two thirds of goals scored come from low shots, so keeping the ball down is the key skill to develop. Our arms go out for balance and our shoulders swivel to generate power, turning in the direction in which our kicking foot is travelling. We have leant slightly forwards to keep the ball low.

For shots we wish to lift, our head is more upright, we do not lean as far forward and our non-kicking foot is planted slightly further back than for a low shot.

Developing our weaker foot for shooting is about making it instinctive. Often, shooting opportunities are fleeting, and require a first time effort. We should work on developing that instinct by spending training sessions giving extra time on the weaker side, even if it means a little practice with a keeper or a wall when everyone else is heading to the bar, or still driving to the training park.

We can practise in our backyard with the kids or, again (and even better, because we can shoot harder) a wall. Keeping a balloon in the house gives an opportunity to have a strike or two when we head to the bathroom, or to make a cup of coffee.

We can have a swing walking down the street, or in a quiet corridor at work. Just make sure the boss doesn't get it on the shin as we plant one into the bottom corner – metaphorically, of course.

In the previous section, we looked at how understanding the strengths and weaknesses of our opponents can make us into more effective strikers. It does not take much thinking to realize that defensive players are making the same calculations about we attack minded players. If we go back to our example from the professional game, we can see how much harder Van Dijk's decision would have been had he known Sissoko was two footed.

He would have to have moved in for the tackle, because he would not have a weaker foot to shepherd his opponent on to. That would almost certainly have led to a simple pass to the supporting Son, and a much higher subsequent chance of a goal ensuing. The importance of being a two footed striker cannot be over-stated.

Top Tip To Take-Away 6 – Sometimes a defender can do no more than reduce the chances of a goal, rather than eliminate them altogether. In these circumstances, intelligent defending is as important as the physical attributes the defensive player possesses.

Top Tip To Take-Away 7 – Parents and coaches should instill the importance of using both feet into the minds of young players as early as they can.

Top Tip To Take-Away 8 – Both feet are important whichever one takes the actual shot. The technique is the same for both right and left footed shooting. There is no reason for being a 'one footed' player, other than it feels more comfortable. Even that is addressed if we practise regularly enough.

Making the Step Over, Drop of the Shoulder and Other Dribbling Tricks a Natural Part of Our Game

A good striker is already going to know whether they have the pace to outrun their defender in a one versus one situation. A speedy winger, or new style 'sprinter' center forward will often have that edge in pace. But not always.

Nowadays, the old fashioned target man has begun to fade away from the game. As a result, defensive players no longer need to be six feet four to win aerial battles. Speedier, more agile defenders are in vogue. All of this combines to mean that offensive players need more than just pace to beat their marker. They need guile as well. The challenges facing center forwards, number 10s and wingers (to which list we must add wing backs) are greater than ever. This is a bigger need in a place like the US, where strong, athletic defenders are the norm.

Let us take a look at a few of these individual skills which we can incorporate into our offensive play.

The Step Over – leaving our defender prostrate on the floor

The Portuguese superstar and frequent Ballon D'Or winner Christiano Ronaldo is master of the step over. Find clips on line of this winger who converted to center forward. What is most astonishing is the speed at which the Portuguese player's feet operate. Whether running flat out, or stopping prior to accelerating away, the step overs occur in a flash of flying feet. Only a moment of confusion needs to flicker in the defender's mind, and Ronaldo is away.

Even from his early days as a teenager at Manchester United, the player was capable of terrorizing defenses. Indeed, Sir Alex Ferguson's decision to play his as a winger, before moving him later into a more central striker position, gave the youngster a chance to develop those skills which still glitter today, even though the player is in his mid-thirties. The stepover has led to countless goals and assists for Ronaldo and his teams and has been one critical factor in his success.

The step over works best when running at high speed, directly at a defender who is dropping backwards to slow us down. However, for those sufficiently talented, it can also be used when we stop, and draw the defender in.

The move is at is sounds. We simply use our foot to rotate over the ball without touching it. The defender follows the foot, his weight shifts and space is created. We then shift the ball with the other foot to exploit this space.

A double step over causes even more defensive confusion. Here, first one foot carries out the maneuver, then the other. The defender is increasingly unbalanced as stepover follows stepover.

The key to perfecting this skill is balance. We work (with or without a ball) on running on our toes, with arms out for balance. We try to complete the foot movements of the step over without losing speed.

Drop of the Shoulder and Goodbye

We can improve this skill without the need for a ball. We can get the movements right before working against a real opponent. This maneuver is about disguise and body movement. We run at three quarter pace towards our defender, the ball under close control, and with us balanced and on our toes.

As we approach the defensive opponent, we dip one shoulder, push our weight that way, drop and bend the knee on that side. We flick the ball in the other direction with the outside of our other foot. Our opponent has followed the drop of our shoulder and shifted their weight that side, making it hard for them to react to what comes next.

As we flick the ball, we push off our planted foot, thrusting from the bent knee. We accelerate after the ball, with our pace changing to top speed. If we have completed the move correctly, we will have wrong footed our opponent, creating time for us to dribble on or get in a shot, cross or pass.

The Cruyff Turn — Memories of a Magician

Some great players have never managed to win the World Cup. Michel Platini, George Best, Lionel Messi, Ronaldo are four who come to mind quickly. But there is another who came incredibly close. That is the maestro who is Johan Cruyff. This midfield genius was the talent behind one of the greatest sides ever, the total football Dutch teams of the 1970s.

Cruyff mastered this little move which is perfect for creating the space for a cross or shot. It involves a rapid change of direction, moving from an almost stationary stance. The attacker's leg is planted between the ball and the defender to protect it. The other foot hooks round and traps the ball. There is a momentary pause, and the ball is then pushed (not kicked, this is a subtle move) at between 90 and 180 degrees from where it had been heading. The attacker then changes direction and sprints away with the ball, shooting or passing if the chance arises.

The Cruyff turn is all about deceiving a defender. Therefore, the attacker uses every ploy that they can to achieve their aim; the arms rotate, the shoulder dips and the eyes mislead. Used effectively, the Cruyff turn is a highly effective tool to help a striker go past his or her defender.

Kids love to learn these skills. They are fun for adults to use as well. To practise, start in a stationary position, unopposed to get the movements and weight of touch right. Then progress to moving at a jogging pace. Finally set up a square of cones 15 yards apart, and work on changing direction at each corner.

Footed Touch – Squeezing through spaces

A defender's job is often to slow down a striker until support arrives to close down space. A striker can create space of their own in this situation with a tricky but effective piece of skill. In effect, he or she makes a short pass with one foot to our other, and then uses that foot to propel the ball through the space between defenders. The striker lowers their center of gravity and accelerates through the space after the ball. Even if the skill does not come off, a free kick will often be won as the defensive players try to close the space.

There are two key criteria required for this skill. Firstly, the striker needs fast feet. Secondly, an explosive change of pace. Players can work on both of these during their everyday lives. Add in short sprints to our everyday fitness plans. The technique requires dropping the center of our gravity, pumping our legs and arms, and driving forwards.

Fast feet improve with lots of short steps. Agility ladders are excellent for this. But there are agility ladders in most streets and in many backyards. They go by the name of paving stones, and are ideal for working on short, powerful steps.

Once we have the physical criteria in place, we can introduce a ball and practice short passing between our feet.

The Nutmeg – How To Annoy Our Full Back

Nobody likes to be nutmegged. This is the move whereby the ball is 'passed' between the defender's legs, and the striker runs around, leaving his or her opponent looking and feeling a little silly.

As defenders jockey their opponents, they will tend to spread their legs for balance and to enable them to change direction. As the ball is passed through them, they will automatically close their legs to try to stop the ball. If they succeed, the ball will often bounce back to the striker, if not, their own balance and ability to change direction quickly is lost. The striker is away. The crowd cheer and the defender fumes.

Knock and Go – Exploiting Pace

Let us finish this mini section by returning to the primary attribute of many attacking players, especially wide players – lightning speed. In this move we trust our legs against our opponent. The defensive player is attempting to slow us down and get support to prevent this maneuver. But we anticipate this, knock the ball past the defender and accelerate around them.

The fraction of a second, we gain while the defender realizes what has happened, turns and gets into a sprint will give us the opportunity to achieve some space and (fractional) time.

In terms of working on this, again it is about developing an explosive change of pace. We can improve on this with technique – getting our bodies low to the ground, shortening our strides and pumping with arms and legs. In turn, we can develop this skill as a part of our ongoing fitness program as well as in specific soccer training sessions.

A little note – as adults we are usually aware that sudden changes in pace put strain on our muscles and ligaments. This is often of little interest to young players, who just want to get on with their playing or drills. It is important that the coach ensures players have stretched and warmed up before working on drills which rely on a change of pace.

To conclude this section on offensive tricks we can employ to improve our effectiveness, let's just remember that soccer is about fun and entertainment. Neither of these are better shown than in the exciting dribbling skills of a player. They can also form a very enjoyable part of general fitness or warm up activities; ideally with, but even without, a ball.

Coaches can enliven simple dribbling and jogging sessions by shouting out moves to try – 'Step over', 'Drop the shoulder', 'Change pace' and so forth.

Dribbling can change games and create scoring opportunities. It also entertains the crowd. And us, as players and coaches. This alone makes it something on which it is worth spending time.

Top Tip To Take-Away 9 – There are many tricks players can employ to beat an opponent in a one v one situation. Practise a variety of them, or defenders will get to know our favorite maneuvers.

Top Tip To Take-Away 10 – Tricks do not work every time; we need to develop the resilience to keep trying even when our attempts are not coming off.

Top Tip To Take-Away 11 – Because these kinds of skill involve sudden, explosive, changes of pace it is important to be properly warmed up before working on them in practice.

Making the Most of the Midfield

Soccer today is a very fluid sport. If we head back to the seventies, perhaps even more recently than that, roles were very much more clearly defined. Or, those who support the changes might argue, restrictive. Starting from the back, the keeper was a shot stopper. As long as he could kick the ball two thirds of the length of the pitch, his footwork was largely unimportant. As we shall see in the next chapter, that is no longer the case.

Defenders defended, attackers attacked and midfielders were either defensively or offensively employed. Life was simple then, It isn't today. In the modern game, players need to be able perform effectively in all areas of the pitch. For example, no longer is the center forward's defensive duty limited to coming back for corners. Now they must close down defenders (the infamous 'high press'), work back and focus on keeping the team's shape out of possession.

When the long ball was king, strikers usually missed out when possession changed hands, the ball punted over their heads; not so any more.

Which leads us neatly onto the role of the midfielder. None of the attributes we are about to describe and on which we will offer tips for improvement are exclusive to players in this position on the park. However, they are most applicable to them.

Making the Ball Our Friend

Being comfortable on the ball is the mark of a truly talented player. Achieving this is a mixture of physical and mental prowess. Players need the skills to keep possession; the physical strength to withstand challenges and the mental strength to cope with the pressure of this crowded area of the pitch.

Keeping Possession – The First Touch

When scouts are looking at the potential stars of the future, the first skill for which they will look is the young player's first touch. That ability to take the ball under perfect control, protect if from predatory defenders and place it so all options – shot, short pass, long pass, dribble – are available.

Yes, we can work on our first touch, and indeed should do so – at whatever level we play – but there is also an innate skill about this particular aspect of the game. When the above mentioned scouts see a player with promise, and that first touch is good, only then they will look for the other attributes – physical, mental, skill wise that offer crucial potential.

Firstly, we need to develop awareness of pressure. Peripheral vision. Dennis Bergkamp was one of the great players of the game. The Dutch master (these players from the Netherlands do seem to be over represented when we look at the greats) had the most exquisite of first touches. Watch him play – sadly now only possible on video, which does not do him full justice - and it is apparent that way before the ball reaches him, he has glanced round and assessed all the possibilities...and risks.

Thus he knows whether to move towards the ball or wait for it to arrive; he knows whether he should lay it off quickly or whether he has time to control the ball and drive forwards; he knows where space is, and to where his team mates are making their runs. Having a good first touch is not an easy skill, but knowing how the game is developing around us makes it all the more achievable.

We can help build that peripheral vision in two ways. Firstly, exercise. Even walking along the street concentrating on what is happening around us will help us to develop our awareness. Take the Beats off, and watch the world. Soon we will see our observational skills improving, and that will improve our awareness on the pitch – getting this wide picture will become second nature to us. Secondly, we can concentrate on maximising our peripheral vision. There is a fun drill which, if practised regularly, will see an improvement in our peripheral vision.

Take a mug and a toothpick. Sit down at home, and focus on an object – something like a photograph or ornament is ideal. Now, keeping focus on the object, place the mug at the extreme end of our vision. Next, while still focussing on the object in hand, try to place the toothpick in the mug. Playing this little game regularly will see our peripheral vision improve.

The same effect is gained by buying a light board of the kind used by opticians – but the hundreds of dollars this costs might be better spent on something that can be more widely used when a toothpick, mug and a little patience delivers the same results.

A little note here – as we get older, our peripheral vision reduces. Maintaining it not only helps us as soccer players, but in our everyday lives as well.

Now our peripheral vision is set to its maximum, and we are used to examining the field around us, we move onto the physical skills of achieving the perfect first touch.

When the ball is on the floor, taking possession with our shoulder towards the ball and on the half turn increases the speed with which we can make the next move. But more important is to ensure that control is good.

We might control the ball with our feet, thigh, chest or head. Whichever, we seek to cushion the ball by giving slightly as it arrives. Then we aim to get it on the floor slightly away from our feet. We get our head up and, where possible, over the ball. Our arms are out for protection and balance.

Many training sessions will donate time to improving first touch, especially when working with younger players. But we can train easily in our backyard. A wall makes a perfect team mate. It both receives our pass and gives one back. Ten minutes a day working on first touch using a wall and the improvement in our play will be immeasurable. Oh, and don't neglect that weaker limb. It won't appreciate being left out, and might seek revenge when we need it most!

Developing Physical Strength

Balance and strength. These are crucial elements any successful midfielder needs. We can develop these with and without a ball. Agility exercises, weights, dribbling runs using cones and mannequins. Our upper body strength is particularly important when we are seeking to develop the power to hold off pressure from opponents.

As good a drill as any for developing upper body strength is the humble press up. However this is only a useful exercise if our technique is good.

- Keep our feet together;
- The legs, butt and back must be straight and remain in line through the drill;
- Clench the buttocks;
- Hands should be directly under the shoulders'

- The head should be kept in a comfortable position and the neck relaxed.

Coping with Mental Pressure in Midfield

These days, with defenders roaring forward to support attacks, the deep lying midfielder often has little protection behind them. Perhaps one center half is positioned to cover in case possession is lost; perhaps one of the full backs is lateral to us; the chances are that everyone else has pushed on.

However accomplished we might be, sometimes we will make a bad pass, or mis-communicate with a team mate. Possession will be lost and we risk conceding a goal if our opponents can transition to attack quickly.

If it happens to the great midfield passers in the world – Iniesta, Modric, Ozil – then it will happen to us. But what we need to tell ourselves is that for every mistake, we will make a good pass, create a golden opportunity or assist with a goal far more often. The net benefit to the team exceeds the occasional error.

It is human nature to dwell on mistakes, to carry guilt for our failings. But strong players do not fall into this trap. Certainly, they review their play, they try to learn from their mistakes and they attempt not commit the same sin again. But it does not stop them looking for the creative pass.

There are many mental strength drills that players can use to help them develop this aspect of both their game…and their personality. We will look at these later. However, it is worth reiterating here that soccer is a team game. As the truism goes – a team wins together, scores together, concedes together and loses together. When a player makes an error, the support of team mates is crucial in enabling them to move forwards.

One of the finest midfielders of recent times was the Liverpool and England leader Steven Gerrard. Liverpool used to be the dominant club not only in England but in Europe as well. And that meant they were the world's strongest team. But times change and when they won the title once again in 1990 their fans could not have imagined that more than a quarter of a century later they would still be seeking their next league championship.

Then, a couple of seasons ago, they had a great team with a super-strong forward line. The battle for the league title was close, but seemed theirs for the taking. Then, late into a game against fellow rivals Chelsea, Gerrard received a straight forward pass in a defensive midfield position. Expecting the usual delivery of a scintillating passer, the defence pushed forward. But inexplicably Gerrard's first touch deserted him. The ball had been on the ground, perfectly weighted. Then to add to his woes, he slipped. The nearest Chelsea striker happily seized the ball, broke away, scored and the title was lost.

Gerrard was heartbroken but the blame for losing the title was not his. Other points had been dropped over the course of the season, chances missed in that game itself. His team mates and fans stood around him – his legendary status continued undiminished and he moved forwards.

There is a lesson there for every soccer player. Small things matter. The first touch is the foundation of every good player, even at the top. Mental and Physical disintegration and a loss of a first touch can have an impact on anyone at every level. Also, mistakes with first touch tend to happen later in the game. It is more difficult to concentrate when your body is tired at the end of the game.

Top Tip To Take-Away 12 – Even the best players need to practise their first touch regularly.

Top Tip To Take-Away 13 – We can develop peripheral vision just walking down the street.

Top Tip To Take-Away 14 – The best passes go to feet. But we should work on our first touch with the thigh, chest and head as well. In each case, the fundamentals are the same

- We check the amount of pressure we will be under when receiving the ball;
- We decide whether our first touch will be to control the ball, make a first time pass or clear the ball;
- We get our body into position;

- If we are looking to control the ball (usually the best and safest option if we have the time to do so) our first touch 'gives' a little, to cushion the ball;

- We get our head in line with the ball, and use our arms outspread for balance;

- If possible, our first touch is taken on the half turn, so we can move the ball forwards quickly;

- The aim is to drop the ball to feet ready to pass or dribble with the second touch.

Top Tip To Take-Away 15 – Physical strength, especially in the upper body, will help with our first touch, as it makes us better at holding off defenders. We do not need complex drills to improve our upper body strength. The humble push up – or even traditional isometric exercises such as pushing straight against a static object – will help us to develop this attribute.

Top Tip To Take-Away 16 – Our first touch will sometimes desert us. The best players do not dwell on this, instead analyze the reasons why their mistake happened, and address the failings which led to it. In fact, this tip is one that applies to just about every error in soccer – we will not express it every time!

Tactical Awareness – Keeping Shape and Making Runs

The midfielder is frequently both an auxiliary defender and striker. As such, the skills of these two areas of the pitch need to be a part of their arsenal.

Certainly as important as the individual skills of the player are the ability to hold shape and discipline. Coaches will work on shape in and out of possession. These days, at the professional level players have the physical fitness and mental strength to hold their shape even when under pressure. This is why the transition stage – the point at which possession is lost – has become so important in the modern game.

What happens at the professional level makes its way down to the amateur game, so has as much relevance to teams playing a Sunday morning game at the park as it does to the finalists in the Champions' League.

The classic defensive line up of two lines of four with two strikers pressuring the ball is very hard to break down. However, during transition it is often the midfielder who needs to make the biggest decisions. They will be the players most likely out of their 'middle third of the park' position, and also the ones who are best placed to fill in for a defender who has pushed forward or (in the case of transition to attack) the one who will break to join his strikers.

Perhaps the greatest exponent of the midfield mastery in recent years is the Spanish player Xavi. His fourteen years with Barcelona and 133 caps for Spain coincided with the greatest years of these two teams. That is not by chance. Xavi was a phenomenally skilled player, with an outstanding first touch. But his tactical awareness was without equal. Not only was a pass success rate of more than 90% an expectation from him, many of those passes were decisive. Yet he was also aware of his defensive duties.

You Tube is littered with clips of his best performances. His role in the 6-2 win over Real Madrid in the early days of Pep Guardiola's reign is one of the best.

Top Tip To Take-Away 17 – Great knowledge of the game, especially reading what will happen next, is a key to the making of a good midfielder. Such a player should instinctively know what to do, and that instinct is developed through watching the best exponents of the game.

Becoming a Dream of a Defensive Player

No Longer a Player Apart – The Goalkeeper

Back in Chapter One we took a brief look at the importance of unintended consequences. We can see one of these in soccer emerging from a change to the law which occurred in 1992. The 1990 World Cup had been something of a disappointment (with surely the worst final of all time, Germany scraping past Argentina with the game's solitary goal.) In the knockout stages there were a frighteningly low 33 goals scored in sixteen games. When it is considered that ten of these were scored in two matches: England v Cameroon and Czechoslovakia v Costa Rica, the opinion that the 1990 World Cup was a bore fest is hard to question.

However, the reasons for this ware many faceted – defenses were more efficient than offenses; the mindset of many teams was not to lose rather than to win. But specifically, a huge amount of time was lost as the ball was passed back to the keeper, who would hold on to it for long periods, roll it out and get it back again. The whole boring process would then be repeated.

Score in the first ten minutes and the game, it seemed, was often over. And so, as a reaction to this, FIFA introduced the back pass rule, which forbade the keeper from handling any deliberately played pass to them.

Initially, keepers would hoof the back passes they now received down the pitch and an aerial battle would ensue. But now, a quarter of a century later, the role of the keeper has evolved. Thanks in large part to the possession based play of the incredibly successful Spanish national side, and the club Barcelona, coaches have begun to realise the value of building from the back and keeping possession.

In order to achieve this, the keeper plays a very big part. No longer is he or she there just to catch a cross or hit a long ball up to the center forward, but instead is frequently the spare man. Indeed, the player needs to be good enough on her feet to draw a striker out of their position, creating space for the ball to be played out.

Counter attacking soccer is much in vogue, and again the keeper is often key to this. He or she looks to play a long, flat and accurate pass to start an attack once possession is regained. They must also do this quickly, before their opponents re-organize.

The Sweeper Keeper

Of course, we can't all be a mixture of Ronaldo and Gordon Banks. Many keepers started in the position when they were a kid because of three reasons. The first two could be taken as complimentary, in a way. Most probably they possessed a combination of attributes – a bit of height and fair athleticism – that encouraged their coaches to place them between the sticks, so to speak. Sadly, the third attribute was not always as positive as the other two. Keepers often ended up in goal because they were not so skilful out on the pitch.

But, it is never too late to start to learn. Being good with one's feet is something we can all develop. There are a couple of simple, key changes we can make to our training processes which will help us in this field.

Firstly, when it comes to training, do the work mostly with the rest of the team. Traditionally, keepers have trained on their own, or been used to help strikers develop their own finishing skills. Keepers who insist that their training work includes everything that their outfield colleagues do will see their own footballing skills develop.

And there will be a bonus from working in this way. Communication with other players will improve because more time is spent with them. Keepers will also get to know, even better than they already do, the strengths and weaknesses of their defenders. Training with the entire team is also, let's face it, more fun that working with just another keeper or a single coach.

Goalies should be demanding that they take part in the five a side games that often happen in a training session – as an outfield player, and not just in goal. They should have a part in the rondo drills (drills weighted with more numbers on one side, and a smaller number of opponents) – again in a creative way, not just as opposition. The team will benefit in the long run.

This does mean that the specific work a goalkeeper needs, such as working on his or her handling, cross taking and shot stopping, for example, needs to be completed as an extra. However, that is a price worth paying if it improves our all-round playing skills.

Which leads neatly on to the second specific work a keeper can undertake to improve their control and passing. Simply, work on them all the time. On top of the fifty high catches goalkeepers take daily from throwing the ball hard and high against the back wall, add fifty wall passes, twenty five with each foot. Work on first touch as well as first time passing.

There is no reason, these days, for the goalkeeper to simply be a presence in the goal, the very best add more than a hoof down the pitch to the creative aspects of their team.

The Schmeichel Star

Danish goalkeeper Peter Schmeichel was rated the world's best player in his position during the early nineties, winning the IFFHS (the International Federation of Football History and Statistics) World's Best Goalkeeper award twice in a row (1992 and 1993) and coming runner up twice more. Given that the title has been won for all but four of the years of its existence by a goalkeeper from a top world force in international football (usually, Spain, Germany or Italy) his achievement is even more remarkable.

Indeed, Schmeichel was one of the main reasons that Manchester United became the most powerful team in the early years of the Premier League in England. He was an outstanding all round keeper, albeit one whose time was prior to the current trend for goalies to be excellent passers of the ball.

However, he developed one particularly effective technique which substantially increased his success rate in one v one situations compared to other goalkeepers. We might call it a 'star', because it seemed as though he grew extra limbs in this situation.

Schmeichel's technique was to approach the striker advancing on his goal in the normal fashion, narrowing the angles into which the attacker could shoot. He then used a technique which maximised the area of his body. Most goalkeepers will try to 'stay big' in these situations by not going to ground too early, which is good technique. However, Schmeical developed the ability to throw his arms and legs as far apart as possible as the striker was about to shoot. Thus, he did not seek to save the ball, rather make a target so large that, more often than not, the ball either hit him, or because his angles were good, flew wide.

It was an excellent method, one that was highly successful in reducing the amount of simple goals his team conceded in one v one situations. Of course, as its success increased, it placed greater stress on attackers, who knew that their effort would face a high percentage chance of being saved. That psychological play on the mind shifted the balance of power. Now it was strikers who were in doubt, and consequently felt pressured and rushed. Therefore, their likelihood of not scoring increased further.

Working on this technique in practice is simple to do. Get strikers to come from different angles, including straight on. Practise getting the timing right, forcing the striker to shoot perhaps earlier or from a less advantageous position than he might like, and work on making the body as large as it can be. Goalkeepers should still be the outsiders when it comes to who wins the duel, but as this technique improves, the balance of power shifts. Soon, it is the striker who fails more often in a one v one, not the keeper.

Top Tip To Take-Away 18 – As a goalkeeper, be open minded to training techniques, and work hard on foot control and passing…

Top Tip To Take-Away 19 – …without forgetting that a keeper's major job is to prevent a goal.

Mr Reliability, Mrs Trustworthy, Master Mindful or Miss Never Mercurial

A winger can be mercurial; while the word is usually seen as a minor criticism – reliability is regarded as a winning trait in whatever aspect of society we live - that is not so for the true creatives. This is something true beyond the green grass of the soccer pitch. Writers, especially poets or playwrights, benefit from the odd raspberry – it gives their best work perspective. The same goes for actors, or painters. And running backs or big hitters on the baseball park. Plus, of course, those most mercurial of soccer players - wingers.

But a goalkeeper must never be mercurial. It might be a position where the exceptional is welcomed, but consistency is regarded as essential. The problem, of course, is an obvious one. When the central midfielder misplaces a pass, he or she has four defenders and a goalkeeper behind them; when the goalkeeper misreads the flight of a shot the consequences are devastating. Usually, a goal is conceded.

A goalkeeper needs to be meticulous. Preparation and organisation are key to his or her performance. A perfectionist nature might be frustrating at work and dangerous in a relationship, but is a handy asset for the person between the sticks.

The tasteless joke below illustrates the point that a good goalkeeper is a creature of habit:

A man is walking down the street when he hears some shouting. He looks up and sees a lady hanging over a balcony, just managing to grip onto the fingers of a small baby. But the child is slipping, and it is only a matter of seconds before he falls to hit the hard pavement forty feet below.

A crowd has gathered, and they are looking up nervously. The man clears a space under the baby. 'It's OK madam,' he shouts. 'Let the baby fall and I will catch him. I am a professional goalkeeper and never drop a cross. The baby will be safe.'

With no other options the woman lets go. The baby falls and the crowd holds its breath. But the keeper is as good as his words. He takes the baby in a perfect two handed catch and brings it into his body. The crowd roars but the cheers dry up in their mouths as the man bounces the baby three times, and dribbles him to the end of the road.

Our point here is that the goalkeeper must be the most consistent person on the pitch. That consistency comes from doing the same things repetitively. It is a position where habits are essential A goalkeeper must also be the most organised player on the park. Which is where we head next.

Top Tip To Take-Away 20 – Repetition is a vital aspect of training for a keeper.

The Organiser

Goalkeepers are leaders. They are often a team's captain. A part of the reason for that is that goalkeepers reach their peak a little later than outfield players, maybe in their early thirties rather than mid to late twenties. Therefore, they are often the most mature player on the team.

But they also must be the most organised, and a key role is for them to communicate those organisational skills to the rest of the team. A goalkeeper who cannot communicate sees the impact of their talent reduced.

Let's take a pertinent example. It is estimated that qualification for the Champions' League is worth in the region of $50-$60 million. More if significant progress is made beyond the group stages. During the 2018 and 2019 season one of the most exciting battles ever took place in the Premier League. With two of the four sides guaranteed a place well ahead, four more teams fought it out for the remaining two places.

With three games to go, just two points separated the four sides. Then came the Easter weekend 2019. Only Chelsea of the four teams managed to secure even a point during that holiday; Manchester United, Spurs and Arsenal all conspired to lose. Closest of all to getting a vital point were Arsenal, and their game was lost due to a catastrophic lack of communication between goalkeeper Bernd Leno and world cup winning center half Shkodran Mustafi.

Of course, soccer is a multi-national sport now, with all the top teams in the main leagues being made up of maybe five, six or seven nationalities. That Arsenal team playing in the match in question, which was against Crystal Palace (a side they would expect to beat) consisted of three Frenchmen, three Germans, a player from Gabon, a Greek, an Egyptian, a Bosnian and an Englishman. Unfortunately, language issues could not be used as an excuse for the breakdown in communication that cost Arsenal at least one point, and probably all three (they were level in goals, and well on top in other respects when the incident occurred). It happened between two of the German players.

This is what sent sixty thousand Arsenal fans into a state of uncontrollable fury, and two thousand Crystal Palace supporters into unexpected euphoria.

A long ball was played forward. Mustafi, facing his own goal, shepherded it backwards from about thirty five yards from goal. The ball was still travelling quite quickly. The defender was protecting the ball from the highly talented but inconsistent Ivorian and star of the Palace team. Wilfried Zaha, a player about whom the term 'mercurial' might have been coined.

Leno, in a good starting position, made a move towards the ball, as though ready to step out and collect it. Then paused. As did Mustafi, who put his arms out to protect the ball from the prowling Zaha. Unfortunately, neither Arsenal player said a word. Leno decided he could not reach the ball before the on rushing Ivorian. Mustafi decided he would allow Leno to collect it, and the nippy striker Zaha neatly side-stepped the German defender, slipped the ball neatly under the German keeper and into the net.

It was a catastrophic error. Really, both players were at fault. Doubly so. Firstly, and relevantly to our point in this section, both players should have communicated – Leno had time to collect the ball, and Mustafi to clear it. It was the goalkeeper who had the best view of what was unfolding before him, since Mustafi had his back to Zaha, although so unexpected was the break through, given Arsenal's dominance, that the defender had more time than he should ever need to deal with the situation.

Secondly, both committed a cardinal sin for their position. If in doubt, kick it out might sound agricultural as a way of playing the beautiful game, but is better than conceding a stupid goal.

So if two international footballers representing one of the strongest teams in Europe, as well as one of the strongest nations in world football can make a silly error like not communicating, then the Sunday morning amateur certainly can as well.

There is no great trick to communicating. The best advice for the keeper is to talk all the time. Effectively, to commentate on the match, instructing defenders constantly. This serves three purposes. Firstly, it helps the defense – the keeper has the best view of an unfolding situation on the entire pitch, since it all takes place in front of her. Secondly, it helps to maintain concentration. No doubt a part of the problem at Arsenal's Emirates Stadium in the match described above could have been that Arsenal were so dominant in terms of possession and territory that Leno had slightly turned off. Constant commentating and instructing helps to maintain focus. Thirdly, talking constantly ensures that a goalkeeper continues to communicate when it is most needed – when their goal is under threat.

Making the Striker Pay the Penalty

Here's a little poser. Which player holds the unenviable record of missing most penalties in the history of La Liga, the Spanish top division?

The answer is, astonishingly, the little maestro and multiple winner of the title of 'World's best player', Lionel Messi. Penalty taking, it seems, is not a straightforward guarantee of getting a goal. Some analysts think that Messi's problem is to do with consistency, or lack of it. He is not always Barcelona's first choice taker; he does not have a consistent run up; it seems like sometimes he is uncertain whether just to strike the ball to his favoured side, or wait for the keeper to commit.

We can take this example and use it to make the case that keepers have a greater chance of saving a penalty (or forcing a miss) if they put doubt into a striker's mind. The best way to do that is to save a few penalties of course. However, moving across the goal line can unsettle a striker; spreading out the arms and legs to make the goalkeeper appear as big as possible, jumping up and down on the spot can distract a striker legally.

Keepers at the higher levels of the game have access to astonishing amounts of data as to the favourite spots opposing penalty takers like to find; their success rate, their run up and so forth. It is unlikely we will have this in the amateur game, but even so there are other things a keeper can do to give them a better hand in the penalty stakes.

The Eyes Have It – Pay attention for an exaggerated look in a striker's eyes; especially with younger players. This can be a sign that they will try to shoot the ball the other way. Subtlety is often not a great asset of the young, and coaches can offer this tip to their goalkeepers.

Putting Your Foot In It – Penalty takers are probably more nervous than goalkeepers when a spot kick is awarded. After all, they are expected to put their penalty away, whereas a save from a keeper is an unexpected bonus. Goalies can look carefully as the striker place the ball. Keep an eye on their non-kicking foot. Often this will point in the direction the ball is to be struck. This is a subconscious move on the part of the striker, and is therefore frequently extremely revealing.

Put Your Foot Down – On a similar theme, a striker will look for a clean strike as they take a penalty. This means that their non-kicking foot will be planted in a way to allow a straight strike from the kicking foot. Therefore, the standing foot will often point slightly in the direction in which the ball will be struck. A fraction of a second's advantage will be gained by the keeper if they can move early, and even more of an advantage if they dive in the right direction. Clearly, a well hit penalty into a corner will still score, but this exercise is all about increasing the odds of making a save, or forcing a miss.

The Elvis Effect – There was no greater swinger of the hips than Elvis. He would probably have been a rubbish penalty taker in soccer, though. His exaggerated swing would give a clear clue to the keeper regarding where the ball was about to end up. Strikers' hips tend to rotate in the direction the ball will travel just before contact is made. Another useful clue to supplement the keepers' list of penalty saving hacks.

Stuttering Towards Goal – A great one here for the amateur game. We like to ape our professional counterparts; that is especially the case for younger players. A trend in the penalty taking game at the moment is for the run up to be stuttering; the aim is to wrong foot the keeper or get them to dive early. However, such an approach means that the taker will be unlikely to generate as much power as with a proper run up. At professional level, players are sufficiently skilled to hit the ball with extreme accuracy so if the keeper does guess right, the ball is still likely to pass them. But at the amateur standard, or youth level, that accuracy is less consistent. Guess right against a stuttering run up and the keeper has a substantially increased chance of saving the penalty because it will be more softly struck. So, keepers, commit as late as possible if your penalty taker has a stuttering run up; the odds will be switched firmly in your favour.

Bend the Laws: It is a huge shame that certain elements of the laws of the game might as well be cast into the aeons of tape for crossbars and long shorts. Just as the encroachment law is rarely applied so the stepping off the line law is more noticeable by its absence than its use. It is as though referees try to redress the advantage a striker holds when taking a penalty by letting keepers get away with advancing off their line. Do it too unsubtly, and even the most myopic of refs is likely to pull us up, but generally a keeper can gain a significant edge by moving forwards just before the striker hits the ball, and then laterally after the shot is hit.

Studying for Success – Clearly, knowing where our opponent is likely to hit the ball gives us a huge advantage. But as we have seen, the kind of statistical breakdown that tells us, for example, that Harry Kane hits sixty plus per cent of his penalties to the keeper's right is limited to the professional game. However, watching penalties whenever keepers can will help them to learn the science of the penalty taker. Use TV, training, video clips and so forth to examine the body language of strikers, and we will start to see patterns emerge.

It's all in the Math – We should never forget the importance of statistics, though. If we imagine the goal is split into three – the left hand side, the right hand side and the center – it does not take too much working out to realise that the area where we are most likely to make a save is down the middle. And strikers hit the ball there far more often than it might, at first, appear. That could be because the pressure of the occasion has got to them, and in order to avoid striking the ball wide, they over compensate and put it straight to the center of the goal. It could be because they think the keeper is bound to dive, and so will strike the ball into the empty central areas. But some studies suggest that keepers who stand up are more than twice as likely to save a penalty than those who dive.

We are less than one hundred per cent convinced by those figures, but certainly, if a keeper sees no other clue to where the ball will end up, staying upright will make a more than satisfactory last resort.

Top Tip To Take-Away 21 – Studying the striker increases the chances of saving a penalty. This includes the time from which he places the ball to the time when he runs in and finally kicks the ball.

Playing For Time – Know the Rules

It is often claimed that there is an abyss between the administrators of the game of soccer and the fans. To any supporter who has paid good money to go to a match, then sat through endless time wasting from a team, that seems a very fair observation. Then, at the end of the 90 minutes, supporters see the referee has added just five minutes of additional time, when the ball has been out of play for at least a third of the half. It is enough to drive soccer fans mad.

We know the scenario. The weaker team scores early, and then spends the rest of the game trying to slow down play to minimise the chance of losing their lead. For example, a simple shot comes in, the keeper catches the ball and in a completely unnecessary way falls onto it. He remains prostrate for fifteen seconds, raises his head and peers around for another five seconds, gets slowly to his feet and ambles at a snail's pace to the edge of the box. Finally, he throws the ball down to his feet and launches it up pitch. At least half a minute has passed since the initial shot came in.

The crowd boo and scream, and the referee continues, oblivious to the frustration of the supporters. Eventually, when repeated once too often at a goal kick, he might produce a yellow card for the keeper. But only after several minutes of potential play have been lost.

Of course, though, the rules of the game do provide for this type of time wasting, at least in part. The goalkeeper has just six seconds from using their hands to control the ball to releasing it from those hands. We suspect that, like us, most soccer fans have never seen this law enacted. However, it could be. The sanction for delaying over six seconds is an indirect free kick from where the infringement took place. Since this has to be inside the penalty area it is a potentially catastrophic free kick to concede.

Most fans would like to see that rule enacted far more often. At professional level, that may be a forlorn hope. However, at amateur level it may well be enforced. The referee is advised to give a warning before implementing the sanction, but does not have to. Keepers beware!

The Stopper Dies, The Playmaker is Born

Those of us who belong certain to a certain age and have played soccer all of our lives will remember how it used to be, especially if we played the sport at school. The coach would take a look, and categorize us accordingly.

'Umm, you're fast, up front; a bit small – full back; you look like you kick it miles – center half.' And the one left ended up in goal. We know a little more these days. While we don't often find a hundred pound center half, nor is it essential to weigh twice that and stand six feet four to hold down the position.

Instead, other skills are important. The ability to organise and communicate, to read the game and, the focus of this section, to create attacks purposefully, rather than hoofing the ball half the length of the pitch and trusting that it breaks to our own side.

However, the way a center back uses his or her footballing skills is different to the way a striker or attacking midfielder might. While good passing, the ability to dribble the ball out of defence and an excellent first touch are all key aspects of the modern center half, they are usually conducted in a scenario where the player has more time and space in which to operate.

It makes sense really. When a striker or number 10 tries an intricate pass it creates a goal scoring situation. But also the risk of losing possession. However, if the worst occurs, there are still plenty of players behind who can win the ball back.

If the center half loses the ball through trying a bit of intricate skill, then the resultant transition is highly likely to turn into a chance for the opposition to score.

Therefore, center backs can improve their play by working on passing and dribbling in low pressure situations.

Top Tip To Take-Away 22 – Develop footwork and ball skills as a player in defense; but don't forget that Row Z of the main stand likes to see the ball occasionally! We will look at this point next.

The Technical Areas on Which a Center Back Needs to Work

We stand by all of the above. Today, a great center half needs to be a proper footballer; not just an effective stopper. However, those old skills are not completely redundant. There are times when the ball has to be won, an opponent has to be stopped and a ball has to be cleared. So, on top of the 'ball' skills talked about above, we would argue that a great center back needs to work, in training, on the following more 'robust' aspects of the game.

Heading: Height and distance are the keys for a defensive header. Players attack the ball, rather than waiting for it to reach them. Arms are held wide for balance, and a 'hen peck' thrust of the neck muscles imparts power.

Center backs are often a target at attacking set pieces. Corners, long throws and free kicks can be directed towards these players. By definition, the center back will often be one of the tallest players on the pitch, and also one of the best headers of the ball. The near post flick on, where the player flicks the ball with the top of their head, is a move that is almost impossible to defend against. It is still one of the most common ways to score from corners.

An attacking power header uses the same technique as the defensive header, although the attribute of height is replaced by direction. Players look to get above the ball to head downwards, and use their neck muscles to direct the ball.

Finally, defenders will sometimes look to head the ball when not under pressure, for example when cutting out a cross field pass. Ideally here, they will look to make a headed pass. Again, the basic technique is as before, with wide arms and spaced legs forming a solid and balanced base. The neck then twists on contact to direct the ball.

Training and Heading: We cannot stress enough the safety elements of heading the ball. The long term impact of heading the ball on soccer players is only just starting to be understood. Jeff Astle, a center forward from the 1960s and 70s, who played for West Bromwich Albion and England, is perhaps the most high profile player whose premature death is associated with heading the ball. The player died early from dementia which is believed to have been caused by repeated blows to the head as he headed the ball in practice and matches.

Until medical teams understand this growing concern more fully, we advise that heading drills are short and limited to never more than ten headers in a session. Technique should be developed using a light ball. Young players should be given even less time heading the ball, unless a very light one is used, and those aged ten and under should not be heading the ball.

Having said that, having good technique is, it is believed, a key to avoiding long term brain damage from repeated headers. That technique can only be developed with practice. It is a catch twenty two situation; players need to practice heading the ball to prevent damage from poor technique, but avoid headers to avert the damage this appears to cause.

Sadly we, along with the whole scientific community at the moment, have no answer to offer for this conundrum. Other than to remember that safety always comes first.

Clearing: As with heading, height and distance are the keys when clearing with the feet. This defensive skill shares many similarities with other sports. To get maximum control on a tennis ball, the shot has to be hit with the sweet spot of the racket. To gain the best accuracy with a shot on the gold course, it is essential to hit the ball smoothly and cleanly.

The best opportunity for achieving these goals occurs when we offer the maximum area of our hitting tool to the ball. The fullest face of the golf club, through a good swing, the largest area of the tennis racket, thanks to good timing.

In soccer, our hitting tool is usually our foot.

The ball should be struck with the maximum area of this limb as possible. By definition, a clearance is under pressure (if it wasn't, the defender would simply bring the ball under control and dribble or pass it out). Therefore, the risk of missing the ball is great. By using the part of the foot with the biggest area to contact the ball, that risk is minimised. Therefore the ball should be struck with the instep. This is true whether volleying a clearance, or striking it from the ground.

Players should practice using both feet. The weaker foot is 'easier' to use when clearing compared to when shooting since power and accuracy are not crucial elements in a clearance. Arms are positioned for balance; the body leans slightly back to generate height and the ball is struck smoothly with a follow through. Defenders do not need to aim for power in the clearance, if the ball is lifted, then that will create time for the defense to re-organise and repel the next attack.

Control and Distribution: However, we will finish the technical skills a defender should look to practice by stressing the importance of using drills to improve first touch, running with the ball and passing. These are especially important for coaches to get into the mindset of young players. Children often see playing 'defender' as simply hanging back and kicking the ball.

If they are to develop into good players as they get older, it is vital they develop the all round skills of the soccer player.

It's All in the Mind

We mentioned earlier that often the captain of a team is the goalkeeper. That is true, but even more often it is a center back. Let us consider the first choice captains of Premier league teams in the recent 2016/17 season. During that period two teams had keepers as their regular captains, three central midfielders and two opted for strikers. An incredible thirteen, or sixty five per cent of clubs, employed a defender as captain. Of those thirteen teams, twelve used a center half in the role.

This position of center back requires leadership, focus and authority. Which are, of course, characteristics of a captain as well.

A center back needs to be able to read the game. Positioning is a key skill, as is anticipation. Per Mertesacker was center half for the World Cup winning German side of 2014. He is affectionately known as the BFG (after writer Roald Dahl's character the Big Friendly Giant). That is because despite his six feet six inches long gangly frame, Mertesacker made a career from reading the game. He was not an especially physical player, and he did lack pace. But he more than made up for this by knowing exactly where to position himself, how to direct his team mates, and how to anticipate what an opposing attacker might do.

A player does not win a world cup without considerable talents and the BFG is a good lesson to any would be defender who feels that they are not quick or aggressive enough to play at the back.

Of course, some players innately understand the flow of a game. Mostly, though, players who read the game well are also experts at understanding the sport. They watch the game relentlessly, study patterns of play and learn the tricks and favourite movement of their opponents.

Using television and video clips helps center backs more than players who occupy any other position on the pitch.

Let's Get Physical

Fabio Cannavaro, the great Italian center back stood only five feet nine inches in his soccer socks. Puyol, the Barcelona central defender stands at just an inch taller, being five feet ten. Nathan Ake is a promising prospect in the middle of the defence for Bournemouth in the English premier league and is the same height. The MLS was won recently by LA Galaxy where A J de la Garza was a regular starter – he is just five feet eight. Markus Ballmert, a highly promising center half who plays in Germany is just five feet seven inches tall.

But what these pocket dynamos of defenders share with their taller peers is phenomenal physical presence. Training with strength exercises, cardio vascular work and aerobic drills is essential if a center half, at whatever level, is to compete in this most physically challenging of positions.

The following specifics should constitute the aims of a physical training programme for a center half.

Strong Lower Body Strength: Center halves need to be strong enough to win tackles and not be pushed off the ball when chasing back.

Strong Upper Body Strength: Sometimes, challenges take place in the air, or shoulder to shoulder. Weights and other resistance exercises help to develop upper body strength to allow defenders to win these duels. It is often said by coaches that in order to win a match, the team must win more of its individual duals than it loses.

Thus we can see that a well-planned and monitored resistance training programme should form a part of a center back's regime, perhaps more so than for any other player on the pitch.

Agility: Many coaches and professionals would argue that agility is even more valuable than pure speed (although that is an attribute that is still important.) An agile player will win the ball before a striker has an opportunity to exploit his pace. Mix that agility with a great understanding of the game, and the perfect center back is almost there.

Therefore, we can see that the training routine for a center back should contain a high emphasis on stretches. Yoga, Pilates and dance are excellent activities to compliment the soccer based elements of training.

Another good warm up activity which promotes agility in a realistic match like situation is backwards running. Here, two lines of cones are set up. Behind one set are the defenders, behind the others are the attackers. The defender sets off a second before the striker and gets in front of them. He or she then jogs backwards, shepherding the striker as they jog forwards.

The players then swap roles and head back to their place behind the appropriate set of cones.

Standing Jump: Center backs should develop their leg muscles to give them good spring from a standing position. When dealing with crosses, both in open play and especially from set pieces, there are fundamentally three ways that a coach might seek to organise his or her defensive forces. Man marking is one method. Here, the defender tracks their opponent. The system works as long as the defender does not make an error or, more often, the striker fails to find space away from their attention.

The second system is zonal marking. Here, defenders take responsibility for an area of the penalty box. Basically, they must win any ball played into their zone. Statistics suggest that this is a marginally more successful system than man marking, although it falls down when the ball played in is especially accurate. Since strikers are running onto the ball they can get extra height in their leap, and also aim to reach the ball in the spaces between the zonal markers.

Because both systems are fallible, many coaches now employ a mixture of the two methods. Here, zonal marking occurs in the main danger areas. Alongside this, the best attacking headers of the ball are man marked to negate their threat.

As we can see, any defender operating zonally will be largely stationary as the ball is played into the box. Therefore, in order to match the height their opponent can reach, they must be able to leap high from a standing position.

Science will tell us that somebody with a running jump will still get greater height, but if their opponent is able to leap high as well, it will be enough to prevent a clean header.

Top Tip To Take-Away 22 – A good understanding of the theory of positional defense will help a defender to become a more effective player. It is not all about winning just winning the ball.

Finding Our Life Partner

Center backs work in pairs. Or threes. A key role for the coach is to find defensive players whose personalities and playing styles compliment each other. It might seem perfect to have two defenders who want to win the ball every time it comes near them. However, while aggression is an undoubted attribute of a good center half, if the players are too alike, the situation is likely to arise where both go in to win the ball, and space is created behind them.

Therefore, a better scenario is to pair a great, determined ball winner with one whose natural tendency is to sweep and cover. Similarly, while it is important that both players are competent on the ball, provided one has an aptitude for creating attacking situations, it works well if the other is merely a good passer who can deliver the ball accurately and with good pace to a team mate. His fellow center back, full backs or deep lying midfielder will drop in to receive the pass, and create the team's forward momentum from there.

The same goes for pace. This is an incredibly important part of today's game, but it might be argued that the good coach looks to pair somebody with considerable speed with a partner of just average speed. The super quick player will then know that they are likely to have to recover a position at times during the game.

However, the slower player (if they are worth their salt on the soccer pitch) will have learned to compensate for a lack of acceleration through developing their reading of the game. Thus, the coach will have created the perfect partnership in his center backs of an ability to dominate positionally, as well as being able to cover bursts from midfield or the ball played in behind the defense.

Next we come to communication in a center half pairing. Again, the confidence to talk and instruct is crucial in all players, especially defensive ones. However, as with other aspects of defense, it is best to choose a pairing where one player is naturally more dominant. This player is the one who bawls instructions to team mates, who pulls players up with their effort is lacking, whose word is law. The other player will be the more thoughtful kind who will have a quiet word with a team mate after an attack has, fortunately, broken down or a mistake has led to a goal.

The last thing a team needs is for two dominant center halves to contradict each other, causing chaos in a tense situation.

As can be seen, the coach's job is a far more challenging one that just selecting the best two players to form a center back partnership.

Top Tip To Take-Away 24 – The best defensive partnership is not necessarily made up of the two best individual players. It is made by the two that complement each other is best.

Tactical Awareness in Defense

We have talked already about the way the game is changing to become more possession based, with every players needing to be comfortable with the ball at their feet.

Many modern coaches (rightly, we would argue) want their defense to play the ball out. To pass along the ground, and make progress by moving up the pitch steadily, perhaps switching play (hitting a pass across the width of the pitch in one or two steps) to stretch their opponents.

We strongly advocate this as a tactical decision on the part of the coach. It is more entertaining for supporters, more enjoyable for players and probably more effective than simply lumping the ball long and hoping.

However, there are times when the long ball might be the best option:

- When the defender in possession fears that they may lose the ball (although, they also need to be given the support to develop the confidence to take risks – this will happen more in training than in matches);
- When the opposing defense is disorganised, and a quick long pass may cause them more difficulties than a steady build up;
- When a speedy striker has the edge in pace on the defence, and a long ball in behind the full backs will exploit this to the full. When Leicester City shocked the world by winning the Premier League in England in 2015/16 one of their best tactics was a long ball in behind the opposing defense. This was often hit to the corners when opposing full backs were drawn forwards, and Leicester's speedy striker, Jamie Vardy, then outran his central defender to get to the long ball first.

The Attacking Defender – Full Backs, Wing Backs and Flying Forward

Remember the days when teams put out two wingers? Players whose job it was to get the crowd to its feet as they raced down the touch line before whipping in the ball for the center forward to rise gracefully, like a fountain bursting from a Geneva Lake, to head the ball home.

There is a rather sad irony that as pitches at all levels have improved in quality, making dribbling a far more attractive proposition for a soccer player, the traditional winger has started to fade from the team sheet. In fact, it is not uncommon for a coach to send out their team with no wingers at all, and it is extremely unusual for a side to feature two of these speedsters.

Manchester City occasionally start with Raheem Sterling and Leroy Sane, but this is increasingly rare – usually the second winger will be introduced if City are chasing a result. Even when the two do play in tandem, Sterling is usually deployed more as a wide number 10 than an out and out winger.

But width is crucial if a team is to attack successfully. Without width, the middle of the park becomes packed with players and there is no space to pass through. It is a defense's dream to face a side who stay narrow in possession. And so the game has developed, as it always does. The wing back has re-emerged.

Jordi Alba is a great example of this kind of player. Deemed too small (at five feet seven) to play as an out and out defender, Alba flittered on the fringes of the Barcelona youth team as a winger. But it seemed like his small frame would mean a top level career would not develop.

Then, a move to Unai Emery's Valencia saw the Spanish coach switch him to a wing back position. Here, his trickery from deep allied to speed in defense and going forward, made him both a serious threat to opposing defences and a real bonus when his own team were under pressure, especially on the break.

Having such a speed merchant in a back four or five meant that the defense would rarely be outstripped for pace. Soon, Alba was back on the Barcelona wish list, and he returned there seven years after they first let him go.

Wing backs need to be blessed with certain attributes. Some of these can be developed through training, others are physical qualities which does mean that not everybody is suited to this position.

Speed is essential. A wing back must have a burst of acceleration which takes them past their own defender. Since they are also primarily a defensive player, they must be able to recover their own position during transition when they have been caught far up the pitch.

A good set of lungs is also crucial, and this aerobic capacity can be developed with appropriate endurance training. Wing backs will be players who run more than most of their colleagues during a match.

But what marks out their need for extreme physical fitness is that they will also spend a lot of that movement in sprints.

A low center of gravity is useful. Not only will they need the agility to twist and turn against opponents, but also respond to tricky wingers when they are doing their defensive duties.

Allied to these physical attributes, a wing back needs the trickery of a winger. Skills that provide this can be worked on in training. Two footed dribbling, the step over, the ability to accelerate quickly – these are the skills of the new generation of wing back. Finally, a good crossing ability is a must have skill. There is little point having got into an excellent wide position if the resulting pass is wayward.

For those with the physical make up and determination to play the position, being a wing back is a really satisfying role on the pitch. Of course, one of the genetic lines of a wing back is a history of full back skills. However, by adding the attacking verve to these defensive attributes, the player becomes even more useful to a team…and ends up with a more enjoyable role to play.

Top Tip To Take-Away 25 – Even attack minded wingers should work on their defensive skills, because one day they might be asked to play as a wing back.

Dealing With A Wizard of the Wing – Watching the Ball, Not the Feet

Admittedly, the readers of this book are, sadly, unlikely to come up against a Ronaldo, or Lionel Messi or Eden Hazard in their prime. These superb dribblers of the ball mesmerise even the best of defenders. But everything is relative. At whatever level we play or coach we will come across players who are, for that standard, highly talented.

How to defend against them without ending up on our backsides with the winger heading off to attack the goal behind us?

There are a number of tricks and tactics defenders use to increase their chances of winning the ball. Aim number one is to harry the opponent to slow them down until support arrives. Then, with back up behind, we can make an effort to win the ball.

Harrying involves backing off the forward, giving them enough space to make it hard from them to knock the ball past us. Staying on our feet, using arms for balance, giving most space to the player's weaker foot, staying lightly on our toes and keeping a low center of gravity to allow a rapid change of direction are key skills to practise in training.

In a straight foot race, a striker will more often than not outstrip a defender; that is the nature of the two positions. However, sprint training and work on lower body strength can help a defender to develop the explosive acceleration that stops the striker going past them. In order to beat a player, the attacker must knock the ball beyond the defender, and it is in this moment that rapid acceleration will halt the offense and win the ball.

However on top of all of these defensive moves, most important of all is for the defensive player to **keep their eye on the ball**. A tricky opponent will use step overs, hints with the eyes and shoulder drops to try to shift the defender one way while the ball travels in the other. The key item to watch is the ball. Whatever moves the striker makes are irrelevant until he or she attempts to take the ball and beat the defense.

Top Tip To Take-Away 26 – Patience is important for a defender; committing to a tackle too early can have catastrophic consequences. Keep your eye on the ball at all times.

Top Tip To Take-Away 27 – The role of a player in defense is evolving. More and more, these players are expected to be creative rather than simply destructive. This is a good thing. Soccer is a game of beauty, not devastation. However, defenders should not lose sight of their primary role – which is to stop an opposing team from creating the chance to score. Defensive drills and training are still important even in an increasingly offensive game.

Physical Fitness

Successful teams score the most late goals. (They also score the most goals during other periods of the game, which is why they are the most successful. But this is significantly so in the last ten minutes.) There is a good reason for this. Pep Guardiola, Sir Alex Ferguson, Arsene Wenger and other top coaches insist that their sides are as physically fit as possible.

Back in 1999, Manchester United were chasing an unlikely treble of League, FA Cup and Champions League. It looked like the last of these would bypass them as they trailed to Bayern Munich at the end of normal time. But two goals in injury time turn their fortunes around. Luck? No, fitness. Supreme fitness counts even more at the end of a match.

At kick off, both sides are raring to go, and the gap in fitness between the sides will be small. By the end of the game, that gap will be much increased – to a match winning extent.

Physical fitness leads to mental fitness. It reduces the chances of injury. Even more importantly, promotes longer life, greater energy and the release of endorphins after exercise gives a sensation of well-being and satisfaction that is addictive.

In fact, the benefits of physical fitness are so considerable that it is hard to see why the entire population does not engage in regular exercise. Of course, it is not as easy as that. Some people find exercise to be fun, many others do not. Creating time to keep fit in a busy schedule is another challenge that prevents some people from getting out in the fresh air, or heading down to the gym.

However, as soccer fans, players and coaches, the chances are that physical fitness is something important to us. As a result, we reduce our risk of heart disease and diabetes; our bones and muscles will be stronger and last longer.

When we exercise, we reduce the risk of mental health problems, and keep our weight under control. In fact, consider the following and share it evangelically with peers, friends and relatives... Exercise will

- Cut the risk of getting type two diabetes by half;
- Reduce the risk of colonic cancer by the same figure;
- Reduce risk of heart disease by more than a third;
- Cut the risk of contracting breast cancer by a fifth;
- Cut the risk of getting depression by a third;
- Cut the risk of falls among the elderly by a third;
- Lower the risk of dementia by a third;
- Reduce the risk of hip fracture among the elderly by nearly 70%;
- Cut the risk of early death by a third;
- Promote a general feeling of well-being;
- Improve mood;

- Make us into better soccer players who enjoy the game more.

The source for these facts is very reliable – the British National Health Service. (Apart, that is, from the final benefit listed, although, no doubt the NHS would agree with that as well).

Specifically for soccer players some activities offer particular benefits.

Running for Soccer Fitness

Every soccer player, coach or fan keen to keep their physical fitness levels at a high standard can find thirty or forty minutes a day to complete an effective jog of around three miles. For soccer specific training, the following points will help us to develop stamina appropriate for the game.

- Find a route that includes undulations – work on up slopes really helps us to develop our aerobic capacity;
- At about two thirds of the run, find a steepish hill and use this for a spell of sprint work. Sprint for thirty metres up the hill, then turn and jog back. Rest for thirty seconds and then repeat. Aim for five sprints before finishing the jog.

Of course, for those who prefer, a treadmill can be used to generate the same environmental conditions. For some who really enjoy their work outs, and can afford gym fees, this a good way of undertaking exercise. However, for most people who find the jogging element of physical training a little tedious, running outside in the fresh air is more satisfying.

Developing Speed and Acceleration

Here is a simple exercise which can be used to help develop sprinting skills. Repeating the exercise three times per week will help to build up speed from a standing start, and acceleration from a jogging position. Reflexes will also be improved as our muscles will be trained to react.

The drill is straightforward, but safety is very important. The exercise involves a drop, and this needs to be from a safe, solid object such as wall bars in a gym. In order to save strain and damage to knee ligaments, it is best to use a floor which gives slightly. Because this drill involves working muscles in the legs hard, and some impact work, it is important to ensure that we are properly warmed up before partaking in the exercise.

From a height of about one metre, jump carefully to the floor. On landing, drop smoothly into a squatting position and then smoothly straighten up. Repeat five times.

A Soccer Player Looks After His or Her Body

My body is a temple. Well, that's a bit of a cliché, an overused phrase guaranteed to invoke a sardonic smile. But there is some truth behind it. If we are not in good physical condition, we will not be able to perform at our best on the pitch if our body is any thing less than a perfect state.

We will look at diet later, but there are a couple of very simple hacks which everybody can follow to help their body to stay in tip top condition. In fact, these two 'exercises' are ones that everybody should follow, whether soccer players or not. These are sleep and rest.

Sleep

The Sleep Foundation gives a clear explanation of what happens to our bodies when we sleep. For about three quarters of the night we sleep in the NREM stage (non-rapid eye movement stage). This lasts for a cycle of around ninety minutes, and includes the most important time of sleep. During this, blood supply to the muscles increases which allows for tissue growth and repair to occur. It is plain to see why this is important for a sports player.

Our energy levels are restored during this part of the sleep process and hormones are released which help with muscle development.

For about a quarter of the night, again operating on a ninety minute cycle, we sleep in the REM stage (rapid eye movement). It is during this part of sleep that we dream, because our brain is active and energy is generated to both the brain and the body. This is the point that we replenish the resources needed for next day performance; the essential role of sleep before a match is clear.

Some people find sleep difficult. As Shakespeare said in Macbeth it is 'sleep that knits up the ravelled sleeve of care' that is 'nature's balm.' Sometimes, for people who suffer from insomnia, proper medical advice is needed. However, the following tips can help to achieve a good night's sleep.

- Avoid visual stimulation in the hour before sleep – for example by turning off our phones;
- Avoid alcohol, which leads to disturbed sleep;
- Do not eat too late in the day;
- Keep the room in which we will sleep cool;
- Avoid caffeinated drinks after lunch;
- White noise apps, reading (from a book, rather than screen) and listening to calm music can also help some people to sleep.

Judging the amount of sleep an individual needs is not an exact science, however as a general rule the following guidelines show that most of us do not get all the sleep we need. Boys and girls from an Under 10 team should ideally be getting ten to twelve hours per night. Teenagers require approximately nine hours and adults should get between seven and nine hours.

Rest

It seems ironic that in a section highlighting the importance of physical activity to promote fitness, we should stress the importance of rest, but it is still important to avoid the fatigue of over exercise. We see even at the professional level that players become physically and mentally tired if they perform too often.

This is why it is wise to organize a personal fitness programme with a professional – perhaps our club's physical fitness expert, or maybe a personal trainer from the gym – to maximise the benefits from physical activity without risking injury or poor performance from over doing it.

Diet

As we saw earlier, Brian Clough was one of the great coaches in the history of soccer. Following his spell with Hartlepool United, mentioned earlier, he went on to manage two unfashionable teams – Derby Cunty and Nottingham Forest, leading them both to domestic honours.

He steered tiny Derby County to the league championship in the early 1970 and on to the semi-final of the European Cup before they were beaten over two legs by some of the most dubious refereeing of all time against Italian giants Juventus. Then the even smaller Midlands club, Nottingham Forest, was led to several domestic trophies by the blunt speaking Geordie (he was born in the tough north eastern city of Middlesbrough). Clough also secured two European Cups for the team as they reached their zenith of achievement in the late 1970s and early 1980s. But how much more might he have achieved had Cloughie (as he was affectionately known) had more than a rudimentary knowledge of diet. Had water been the way to re-hydrate, rather than beer. Had chicken and pasta replaced greasy fish and chips.

Nutritionists of today will endure nightmares just thinking that professional sportsmen should put such food as Cloughie bought for his players into their body. The idea that just the lower league teams had this idea of diet holds no water (rather like the players) either. It was common place right up to the 1990s for English footballers to celebrate victories or mourn defeats with a hearty fish and chip supper, frequently washed down with pints of warm British beer.

Indeed, it was not unusual for there to be a heavy drinking culture at clubs. Two of the biggest teams in the world, Arsenal and Manchester United, both suffered from this in the late 1980s. Indeed, it was a mixture of the visionary ideals of Arsene Wenger combined with a growing influx of European players who treated their bodies with rather more respect that led to a more professional approach when it comes to diet. Indeed, the former Arsenal, Monaco and Grampus Eight manager once said: 'Food is like kerosene. If you put the wrong one in your car, it's not as quick as it should be.'

Of course, we are not professionals. Our lives cannot be controlled by what we should eat to best prepare for our weekend outing on the football pitch. Nevertheless, we can follow a few simple rules which will help us to keep our bodies in good condition, all the better to keep up physical and mental stamina at the weekend.

Seventy per cent of any athlete's diet should be carbohydrate. This is a lot more than most people eat. An active sports player, training hard a couple of times per week and with light work, such as jogging, on other non-match days, should aim to consume between 2400 and 3200 calories per day. This is a lot more than most players take in. The result is that performance tails off quickly because the body runs out of fuel to power the muscles.

The fuel is best taken on board through frequent but small snacks, rather than in three large meals. Replenishing carbohydrates after exercise or matches is also very important.

Best foods for a soccer player include rice, bread, pasta, cereals, fruit and vegetables. Dairy products in moderation provide valuable vitamins and minerals. Seeds, peas and beans provide essential fibre. Soccer players' protein is best sourced from foods such as milk, eggs, fish, yoghurt and chicken, while food cooked in sunflower or olive oil provides sufficient levels of unsaturated fats. Salmon and nuts are good sources of this food type as well.

All athletes should stay well hydrated, consuming plenty of water.

Snacks from bananas, muesli bars, milkshakes and fruit are good, as are (perhaps surprisingly) bagels and crumpets.

Doctor Hector Uso has worked with successful Spanish La Liga club Villareal, and he recommends the following as a good diet to consume before and after a match. Here are his tips:

- The last meal before a game should be heavily carbohydrate based (for long lasting energy) with just a little protein. Too much protein can cause digestion problems.
- Rice or pasta are the best sources of that carbohydrate, and a small amount of fish with vegetables compliments this well.
- It is best to leave at least three hours between eating and playing.
- After the game it is important to eat within thirty minutes of playing. This is because muscles have exhausted their energy supply and need a burst of glucose and carbohydrate. Pasta or rice are once again the best sources for this replenishment.
- As with before the match, the post-game meal should also include some protein to help prevent muscle problems later. Tuna, chicken, turkey or eggs are an ideal source of this protein.
- Water is an excellent drink, but an electrolyte solution such as Gatorade or Lucozade is even better, as these contains minerals and sugars which the body uses up during intense exercise.
- Fluid should be taken on board before, after and during matches and training sessions. This helps to avoid cramps caused by dehydration, and excessive tiredness - physical and mental). However,

little and often is the rule of thumb with fluids. Drinking too much leads to stomach problems and a feeling of being bloated.

Look after our bodies by controlling what we put into them and we become healthier, fitter and mentally more robust. And as the paragraphs above indicate, maintaining a healthy diet neither has to be expensive nor especially tricky. Common sense and a little care are together enough to ensure that our diet assists our sporting aspirations.

Top Tip To Take-Away 28 – The importance of exercise – for soccer and life – cannot be overstated. However, it is not everybody's favorite way to spend an hour. Exercising with a partner, competitively or in the fresh air help to make it more palatable.

Top Tip To Take-Away 29 – Amateur soccer players can maintain a good diet without having to dedicate their lives to achieving it. Eating and drinking sensibly, in moderation and eating a variety of foods will achieve their aims.

It's All In The Mind

Let us think of the greats of soccer history. In the late 1990s and early 2000s many would make the case that world's greatest player was the magical Frenchman, Zinedine Zidane. Unfortunately, Zidane is not best remembered for his astonishing natural talent, or to his commitment to the French team, with whom he won the world cup in 1998. Nor for the 108 caps he won representing his nation, or the glittering career he enjoyed with Real Madrid as both player and, later, coach.

It is that headbutt in the 2006 cup final that, sadly and wrongly, most defines this astonishing former player. It was Zidane's last game – he had announced his retirement before the competition. Few expected France to do particularly well. Their magnificent team of the latter part of the previous millennium was breaking up, and their progress to the final surprised many.

Once there, they took the lead against a hardened and cynical Italian side with a penalty nonchalantly put away by the maestro Zidane himself. However, Italy manufactured an equaliser and the game went into extra time.

Marco Materazzi was a tough tackling center back, known for a provocative temperament that led him to receive no less than twenty five red cards during a playing career that spanned ten teams and forty one international caps. During the final it might have been expected that he would have been in an upbeat mood. It was he who had scored the equaliser which took the final into extra time. Later, he would score again in the penalty shoot out which saw the trophy head to Italy.

Video footage shows the Italian defender grasping Zidane around the chest with the ball nowhere in sight. The attack breaks down and the two players separate with words exchanged between them. Then, Zidane turns and headbutts Materazzi forcibly in the chest. Not hard enough to provoke the response the defender gives. Seeing the head butt coming, he throws himself backwards, clutching his chest as though shot from close range with a double barrelled shot gun. (Materazzi soon recovered once Zidane's red card was issued.)

Later, it became apparent what words were said: those from Materazzi were racist, insulting, offensive and unnecessary. Still, world football, through the uncertain auspices of FIFA, tolerates racism in a way that is impossible to behold in the educated world even in the dregs of the second decade of the 21st century; back in 2006 it was hardly considered as an offence, which is an appalling indictment on the leadership of the game.

Apparently, Zidane had said ironically to Materazzi as they parted: 'If you want my shirt so much I'll give it to you after the game.' To which the defender replied, on his own admission, 'I'd prefer your whore of a sister.' In fact, Zidane claimed that the defender also insulted his mother, and it certainly seems from watching footage that he said more than just these words. However, what he admitted to was bad enough. Nobody wants to hear their sister described as a 'whore'; to a Muslim like Zidane the phrase is even more offensive. Even Materazzi admitted later that he had perhaps gone too far. 'It's not a particularly nice thing to say, I recognise that,' he said, although he qualified the admission of fault by adding 'But loads of players say worse things.' That's ok then!

Whether the referee heard the comments towards Zidane, and whether if he did it would have made any difference is hard to be sure. In reality, Zidane did commit violent conduct and as such deserved a red card, The guilty, worried look on his face told as much as he realised his final performance in the show piece game of world soccer was going to end prematurely. Materazzi received a two match ban later, but by then he had played a significant part in helping Italy to win the trophy. Certainly, he deserved a red card more than Zidane, but got away with his misdemeanour.

The point of this story is that, justifiably or not, Zidane allowed his mental discipline to fail, and this impacted potentially on the destination of the world cup, and the reputation he earned following a glittering career that deserved so much more.

When we lose control in our amateur game, or make a mental error which leads to a goal being conceded, our failure is something less public than Zidane's. Nevertheless, avoiding such a situation is an aim to which every soccer player subscribes.

Before we look at some of the tricks and hacks we can use to develop mental strength, we will try to put this somewhat nebulous term into a more solid idea by defining exactly what we mean by 'mental toughness'.

The Different Aspects to Mental Toughness

We can break down the concept of mental toughness into the following constituent parts. Each is a characteristic we try to instil into ourselves, or our teams, without taking away the fun of playing. Competitiveness is important, but for every winner there must be a loser in soccer. Sometimes, a will to win at all costs takes away that pleasure that everybody should take from the game, and it ceases to be an enjoyable sport. Instead it turns into a hotbed of pressure in which winning is a requirement that gives no satisfaction, and defeat is a catastrophe that seeps into other parts of our lives. Perspective is all.

Here is one detailed definition of what is meant by 'Mental Toughness':

- *A desire to succeed* – Note, the word is 'desire' not 'need'. Meeting a desire is pleasurable; meeting a need simply sustains life.

• *A commitment to training* – Most players will give their all in a match situation, because that competition is the main reason we choose soccer as our pleasure rather than, say, jogging endlessly on a treadmill. That commitment is harder to sustain in a training session, when the end goal is a step removed from the pain we endure as we push our bodies to their limit.

• *Task orientation* – This is a more technical element of mental strength. Goals are more easily achieved when they are short and specific. To have a 'good game' is a vague objective shared by all players who play soccer, or any competitive sport for that matter. However, defining such a vague statement is hard. Does having a good game mean scoring a goal? If so, what if the team still lose? Or we score one but miss five easy chances? Short, definable goals help us to orientate our minds towards achieving simple steps. 'I will chase down the goalkeeper, although I have only a ten per cent chance of winning the ball'; 'I will concentrate on not losing my man when defending a corner.' These are the kind of short and simple goals that, combined over the ninety minutes of a match, enable us to succeed in meeting that nebulous concept of a good performance.

• *Attention to Detail* – Concentration throughout a game is an important element of sustaining mental strength. If we are careless with a simple pass, we may take the pace out of an attack; if we lose concentration while defending a corner, our man may find space and score against us. Maintaining the mental strength to succeed during the game is as tiring as keeping physically on the move throughout the ninety minutes.

- *Bouncing Back* – A really important part of being mentally strong here. Inevitably, during a game, things will go wrong. Soccer is a team game with many constituent parts. The only one of those we can control is ourselves. Therefore, goals will be conceded, referees will make bad decisions, we will mis-time tackles. The ability to accept such adversity as both inevitable, but also something we can overcome, is central to our mental strength.

- *Consistency* – This is a theme on which we have touched already. That ability to perform well throughout a match, and repeat that level of performance in future matches is something that marks us out as a strong player.

- *Confidence* – Linked to the ability to bounce back, we should believe in ourselves. If we do not think we can make that pass, then we will never try and the team suffers as a result. If we do not think we can recover to make a tackle, then our opponent will go on to score even though they stumble, and lose control and would have given us the chance to make an interception had we believed in ourselves.

- *Motivation* – If we do not have the desire (but not need!) to win, to have pleasure in the game, to try our best, then there is little point playing, and we should be looking at other ways to fill our time or maintain our physical fitness.

- *Flexibility* – This is often a challenge when coaching young players. Most think that they are a center forward, a number 10 or a winger. As young players, they should try out many positions, and learn the challenges and opportunities that each presents. If our mindset runs along the lines of 'that presents an opportunity to learn a new way of playing' rather than 'I'm not playing full back because I am defensive midfielder...' then we both improve as a player and help the team. We also make the role of the coach easier to perform...which might stand us in good stead further down the line.

- *Leadership* – Not every player can be the captain, but that does not prevent every player from showing leadership. On top of this, the nature of leadership changes with time. Thirty years ago, the captain of the soccer team was a fearsome individual, who led because everybody was afraid of doing anything other than follow them. Today, leadership is more subtle. It is about getting the best out of each player. Some respond to a good old fashioned 'bollocking'; others need encouragement, or an arm around the shoulder. The best leaders win respect by respecting their team mates, and are therefore more likely to be followed when the going gets tough.

- *Organization* – We might like to think that forgetting boots or turning up at the wrong time is the mark of a disorganised under twelve player. Most of us will be able to recognise, though, such traits in adults as well as children. Some people do find organization difficult. With regards to the simple things, such as having the right kit, or arriving at the correct time for a match, then a list posted on the front door can provide an excellent aide memoire for those who need it. A box kept by the door which contains everything needed for the day also works. (It can be for soccer kit at the weekend, and work books during the week!). However, being organized is about more than just turning up with two matching socks. Organization is needed on the pitch. The same people who struggle with remembering their kit are the ones most likely to find it difficult to keep their positional discipline when possession is lost. Recognising this can help both the coach and the player. Understanding that being organized is a personal challenge makes overcoming it much more likely.

- *Composure* – 'Ice runs through his veins…' or 'her nerve never falters…' announces the cliché infected commentator. Indeed, some people do seem to be calm under pressure. A little adrenalin boosts performance, maximises the effectiveness of muscles. It focuses the mind and speeds the reactions. Too much, and tiredness descends, reactions slow and confidence oozes away. After all, adrenalin is the chemical our brains pump through our bodies when we face the 'fight or flight' scenario. Some people are naturally cool under pressure. For most of us, though, we can undertake breathing exercises and visualization techniques to help us control ourselves in high pressure situations.

- *Resilience* – Last and most important. Players who develop resilience in sport transfer that vital attribute to every day life. This is one of those many ways in which sport helps us in our every day living. However, resilience takes many years to develop, and for those without it there is no quick fix. Confidence and belief in oneself; a sense of perspective (playing a bad back pass which leads to us conceding a goal really is not the end of the world, however bad it might seem at the time) and a mindset that sees every set back as an opportunity for spring boarding new growth. These are the mental conditions which sit behind resilience. But lack of resilience can be traced back to many events none of which may be connected with sport. Childhood catastrophes, bereavements, bullying...there are so many reasons why a person might lack resilience. All that we can do as team mates, coaches and friends is seek to build a player's self-esteem. A person who believes in themselves copes with failure. Indeed, the most resilient people do not recognise failure; something going wrong is simply the first step towards making something better.

Some Simple Ways to Develop Mental Strength

Our detailed breakdown of what constitutes mental strength has offered some simple tricks to help us improve this part of our game. Here are a collection of other drills and activities that can help us to develop mental strength through improving one or more of the attributes listed above.

Trust the Law of Attraction

This theory works on the principle that like minded personalities are attracted. Therefore, a person who is positive in their outlook tends to mix with others who are forward thinking and creative. As a result, through sharing ideas in talk and activity, that positivity is increased. With positivity comes the willingness to take risks, resilience, confidence and self-esteem. Conversely, negative people tend to attract other cup half empty personalities and a vicious circle of downward attitudes develops. Therefore, people should actively seek to be positive, using complimentary and congratulatory language. Each challenge can be viewed as an opportunity, not a threat.

Analyse Our Own Performance

It can be tough to reflect on a bad performance…but not if we see such analysis as a positive exercise. We can consider the reasons why the opposing winger constantly got in behind us (should we try committing forward a little less often? Could our communication be better?) Then, we can talk with team mates to try to find ways to resolve the problem. Thus, the 'failures' of the game become starting points for making us into better players.

This kind of analysis is something that can be used by a coach as well. The best coaches use positive language which encourages involvement of players. Rather than 'You should have passed rather than shoot in that situation' try something like 'what was the best option in that situation?' Then, rather than making a player feel bad about their performance, and damaging their confidence, they are involved in seeking ways to improve their play.

Focus On the Present

The past is done and cannot be undone, the future is dependent on what we do today. If we stay in the present, we are more focussed and therefore mentally more concentrated.

Develop Focus

Sport is a competitive activity, so sometimes things go well, and frequently they do not. It is easy to dwell on the past, which is a characteristic of those with poor resilience. A small drill, called the Four Rs, can help with focus in training and match situations.

Release, Relax, Revise, Refocus

Release – It is perfectly acceptable to release emotions after something has gone wrong. It gets the frustration out of our system quickly. Remembering the importance of sportsmanship, such a reaction should never be detrimental to others, but will give us the first step towards getting our focus back on the game.

Relax – Breathing exercises will help us to relax; now we have released our emotional surge as well, that relaxation will be easily achieved.

Revise – This is a personal part of the process. We develop a system that works for us to get back on track. For example, for a soccer specific situation, we may have just been roasted by a tricky winger. We might therefore tell ourselves firmly that this will not happen again. 'I can stop her from going past me!'. Visualisation is also a powerful tool. We picture in our mind us dropping a little deeper and harrying the winger for longer, rather than diving in as we did, unsuccessfully, a moment ago.

Refocus – This is like a restart button and should use an external cue, unrelated to the situation in hand. So, for example, we may have a key word that reboots our mind. Perhaps a favourite food, a partner or loved one. We could use a pictorial reset button. For example, the beautiful beach we visited last summer. There are two key points to use with this refocussing technique: firstly, we should know in advance what that cue will be – we do not want to be distracted by having to think of one at the very time we need it most, plus the repetition of using the same button will make the process stronger in our minds. Secondly, the button needs to be extremely simple. Again, we do not wish to waste valuable time and energy working out something complex, like a riddle or a three stage visualisation.

Keep a Mental Journal

This trick does in some ways contradict the concept of living in the present. However, since it is a method to help us get back to the present, and retain our confidence, it can be allowed!

Our journal can get bigger over time, but once something is written mentally inside, it never goes away. We can start our journal with a little literal preparatory work. We think of three examples when things have been going against us, but we have overcome them. We write these down. We then read our written words and create images for them which we stick in our minds.

We then refer to this mental journal of success when we need a burst of confidence. For example, when we are about to take a penalty, or before the kick off of an important match.

Visualise A Stop to Negativity

This is a simple yet great little trick to help us overcome negative thoughts which might creep into our thinking.

Every time a negative thought enters our mind we picture a flashing red stop sign. At the same time, we state the word 'STOP!' firmly in our head. This helps to break the negative thought processes and allows us to refocus on the task in hand.

Build A Mental Manual Of Success

Spend some time thinking about what represents good play in a given situation. That can be physical, mental or technical. Often it will be all three. Think of the key elements that will make that situation a success. Write them down and learn them. For example – when shooting think 'head over the ball' and 'aim for the corners'; practised enough these thoughts will become second nature, and help us to perform with physical accuracy in a pressure situation.

It s easy to disregard the importance of mental strength in sport. However, if we are to be successful soccer players then mental fortitude is at least as important as strong technique and physical strength.

Top Tip To Take-Away 30 – We have looked in a lot of detail at what constitutes mental toughness, and ways to improve it. Therefore, we will finish with this simple point, which can become a mantra in our search for soccer related betterment: Mental toughness is at least as important as skill and strength in the make up of a talented soccer player.

Learning From the Best

Head into any school, or visit any youth sports team and ask for a list of favourite players. It will not be an especially diverse list. When it comes to soccer, the likelihood is that the name Lionel Messi, or Ronaldo, or Neymar will feature widely.

As we get older, we learn more of the subtleties of the various players that make up a team. But it is still fine to have a favourite player. We can learn from that soccer expert.

Choosing Our Role Model

If we are to learn from watching a master professional ply his or her trade, then we need to pick that genius carefully. Video clips are a useful tool, but tend to focus on the most spectacular aspects of a game – great shots, passes and so forth. Not the everyday elements of soccer that, performed consistently and with quality, turn the average player into an outstanding one. To learn about these, we either need to see the player live, or regularly on TV.

That means that the player either needs to play locally, so we can go to see him in the flesh, or for a big European side who feature regularly on TV. Probably the easiest soccer to watch on TV in the US is the English Premier league. Many readers will have their chosen teams and players already; however, for youngsters who we want to get into the game, and for older players who have no particular favourites, here is a list of some of the best players in each position who, at the time of writing, are plying their trade in the Premier League. We have chosen players in the early or middle part of their careers, so they will be going strong – injury permitting – for a while yet.

Strikers

The Old Fashioned Center Forward

The traditional target man is fading from the game, and the number nine needs to be more versatile than in the past. **Dominic Calvert Lewin** is an up and coming striker, a big and effective target man who also possesses good dribbling skills and pace. He plays for Everton. **Romalu Lukaku** is Manchester United's Belgian target man. As well as having enormous physical strength, Lukaku is worth watching for his strong running skills, especially when he can get onto a one v one situation in and around the penalty area.

The Free Scoring Wide Player

Liverpool, under the leadership of the effervescent Jurgen Klopp, have enjoyed a resurgence in recent years. Much of this has been based on their devastating strike force of **Roberto Firmino** (who we will look at later), **Mo Salah** and **Sadio Mane**.

The latter two of this trio tend to play on the left and right of attack, and use their pace and running skills to advance into goal scoring positions. Both are prolific net finders, hard to mark and natural finishers.

The Link Man Center Forward

So onto the third of Liverpool's men of the moment. Brazilian **Roberto Firmino** typifies the striker of the modern game. He is multi-talented and able to play anywhere across the front line. He possesses the passing skills and vision of a number 10, the pace of a winger and is a natural goal scorer. For anybody looking to watch the master striker of today, Firmino presents a perfect role model. We can learn huge amounts from his work off the ball as well as when it is at his feet.

Firmino (along with Salah and Sane) is also the first line of defence for Liverpool. Not for him defensive duties limited to heading away corners and free kicks, his role is to close down when the opposing defense has the ball, forcing them into errors and turning over possession quickly. Such a task requires immense levels of physical fitness.

The Number 10

Many would say that this position is often filled by a team's most talented player. We will use the example of **Raheem Sterling**, the up and coming Manchester City forward to illustrate this role, and the way it is adapting in the modern game. Sterling is a fine passer, able to find space against a packed defence (an absolute must have skill) and a good finisher. He is also, as coaches like in a Number 10 these days, able to play wide as a winger (his original position) or as the main striker. Such flexibility gives the coach options with his formation and creates added difficulties for defences, as the player is able to wander into different positions.

Midfielders

The Number 8

By this, we mean the midfielder who is a box to box player, as adept at supporting the defence as he or she is at bursting into the penalty area to put away a well-timed pass. This kind of player must be a good reader of the game, extremely fit (it is probably the position that requires most running) and with a good eye for goal.

One of the best perpetrators of the position at the moment is the Wales and Arsenal midfielder **Aaron Ramsey**. He is soon to move to Juventus and will be an extremely hard player to replace for the north Londoners. Ramsay scores some great goals – and also important ones.

Twice, he has scored the winner in a cup final. It is rare that, at the end of the game, he has not run further than any other player on the park.

The Play Maker

Often, this role is filled by a Number 10, although the position can be occupied by a central midfielder. The Spurs and Denmark master passer **Christian Erikson** is a good player to watch for those who want to improve in this job. He reads the game extremely well, can pass short and long with accuracy and also chips in with crucial goals. Young players can see how he works hard when to find space when Spurs win the ball. Teams set out to close him down quickly, to prevent him causing damage with his range of passing, but Erikson is a master of avoiding the attentions of defensive midfielders.

The Wide Midfielder

This position is the evolution of the winger. With the emergence of wing backs, many teams avoid using a winger as their way of creating width, instead requiring the job to be shared between the wing back and wide midfielder. This player also has defensive responsibilities, needs to be a good passer and dribbler and has an eye for goal.

Ryan Fraser is a Scottish international who plays for Bournemouth. It seems only a matter of time before he earns a move to a leading European team. Fraser is the archetypal wide midfielder; a devastating runner with the ball, his defensive skills are also excellent.

The Central Defensive Midfielder (CDM)

Lucas Torreira is a diminutive pocket battleship from Uruguay who anchors the Arsenal midfield. We can all learn a lot from watching him play. Torreira reads the game well, and seems to find himself always in the position to break up attacks. Despite his small size, he is a ferocious tackler (his low center of gravity helps here), a fine passer and a player with an eye for goal and a powerful long shot.

Defense

The Center Back

We have talked already about the mighty **Virgil Van Dijk**. However, such is the stature of the Dutch defender that we really can do no other than use him as a role model for this crucial position. Sadly, few of us possess the range of attributes he has, but because he can do it all, we can use him as an example through which we improve our own speciality play, and also learn about other aspects of defense from him.

Firstly, Van Dijk is tall, strong and quick. This gives him a physical advantage which we may not be able to replicate. However, his excellent ball skills and passing range is something on which we can work.

Van Dijk also reads the game extremely well. We can learn a lot from watching his positioning as plays develop. He is also a great communicator, which is a crucial skill for any position on the pitch, especially the center of defense. The Dutchman also brings an attacking threat to set pieces with his aerial ability.

However, perhaps his biggest attribute is that he improves the team mates around him. We spoke earlier of the importance of a complimentary center back pairing. With Van Dijk beside them, that seems to be anybody.

The Wing Back

We will look at another Liverpool player first for this exciting position. **Trent Alexander Arnold** is a fine young player with a great future. He is not the finished article, and that also helps us learn, since we can see when he makes positional or strategic errors. However, he has pace, a remarkable ability from dead ball situations and is a good dribbler and crosser..

The Arsenal left wing back **Sead Kolasinac** is another player worth watching for the wing back position. The Bosnian, along with his partner on the right hand side of the pitch, **Hector Bellerin**, provides the wide outlet for an Arsenal team that rarely includes traditional wingers.

Both Bellerin and Kolasinac are devasting going forward. To study a more defensively minded full back we can turn to Manchester City's **Benjamin Mendy**, the young French defender. Still good in attack, Mendy is more in the traditional mould of full backs, solid in defence with a good reading of the game. In a time when most full backs have converted to wing backs, he is one of few young players performing as a traditional full back for a top team.

Goalkeeper

We would recommend that would be goalkeepers look at two keepers who between would make the perfect man between the sticks. Manchester United's **David De Gea** is a superb shot stopper, with astonishing reflexes and handling. His positional sense is second to none, and means that often shots that would require scintillating dives from other keepers, he simply plucks effortlessly out of the air. In contrast, **Ederson,** Manchester City's Brazilian, represents the new breed of goalkeeper.

If De Gea is a super traditional keeper with good distribution skills, then Ederson is a good keeper with an outstanding ability to control and pass the ball.

There are many other brilliant exponents of every position and type of player who we can watch on TV. Players in Europe, South America and the US itself make excellent role models from whom we can learn technique, positioning, mental strength and the importance of physical strength.

We learn from observing the best, and the place to find the best when it comes to analysing performance is the television. We highly recommend taking out a subscription. The analysis by pundits that takes place at half time and after the game is also a brilliant source for learning about the game. Where else, but on TV, could we have ready access to some of the world's finest soccer brains?

Analysing the performances of professionals will make us more informed about the game in the widest sense. Hence, we will become more effective players.

Conclusion

Pep Guardiola is probably the world's leading coach. Having gained enormous success with Barcelona, Bayern Munich and Manchester City, he is a manager from whom we all can learn.

'Talent depends on inspiration,' he once said, 'but effort depends on each individual body.'

His words might not hold grammatical perfection, but they do send an important message. One that says we are the secret to our own soccer success. Whatever talent we might be born with, whatever physical attributes we might possess, our final standard as soccer players will depend on the effort we put in.

We play soccer for pleasure. That pleasure comes with the added bonuses of promoting physical fitness; of generating mental well-being; of establishing opportunities for friendship which can be life long. Those benefits are greater when we really commit to our soccer.

We hope that this book has given a broad and varied insight into some of the hacks and tricks that can help us to maximise our potential as soccer players. Perhaps these can be summed up under a small number of headings:

- Technical skills maximised through training;
- Physical skills perfected through a regime of fitness training;

• Mental strength which supports us not only in our soccer playing, but in wider life as well;

• The importance of communication;

• The importance of reading the game. This can be learned through studying matches and watching the very best exponents of the sport.

Good players will already use many of the tips and hints, strategies and techniques we have outlined in this book. There are a limited amount of ways to play the game, and for experienced players the challenge is as much about improving consistency and precision with existing skills as developing new ones. Nevertheless, it is always handy to recap on the essentials of the game. In addition, we hope that every soccer fan – player, parent or coach – will be able to take something with which they can improve their own game…and their enjoyment of it.

Love this beautiful sport – it is the best in the world. It is also the most popular, and one of the easiest to play. A ball is all that is needed.

The skills and strategies we have highlighted in this book will help to make us even better performers, and therefore improve our enjoyment of the greatest game on the planet.

CPSIA information can be obtained
at www.ICGtesting.com
Printed in the USA
LVHW050036090621
689708LV00012B/1385